D1061921

DIAGRAM SHOWING HOW WE GOT OUR BIBLE.

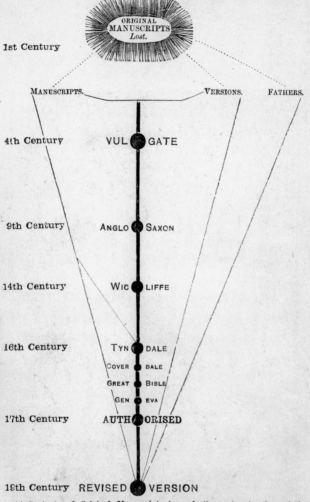

1st Century   ORIGINAL MANUSCRIPTS *Lost.*

MANUSCRIPTS.   VERSIONS.   FATHERS.

4th Century   VUL GATE

9th Century   ANGLO SAXON

14th Century   WIC LIFFE

16th Century   TYN DALE

COVER DALE

GREAT BIBLE

GEN EVA

17th Century   AUTH ORISED

18th Century   REVISED VERSION

(1) Contents of Original Manuscripts (now lost) survive in the existing MANUSCRIPTS, VERSIONS, and FATHERS. (See p. 16).

(2) The Latin Vulgate (a revision of the Old Latin *Versions* by comparison with Greek and Hebrew *Manuscripts*) is the source of our English Versions down to Tyndale. He first draws from *manuscript* sources but of modern date.

(3) The three sources — MANUSCRIPTS, VERSIONS, and FATHERS — are all combined for the first time in the recent Revision.

Photograph of ANCIENT GREEK Manuscripts :—

1. Scrap of a famous Greek Manuscript of Genesis. *(Codex Geneseos.)*
2. Portions of its writing, full size.
3. Fac-simile of the Alexandrian Codex in the British Museum (see p. 27).
4. A portion of a 9th Century Manuscript.
5. Beginning of 29th Psalm on Papyrus in the British Museum.

Facing Diagram.]

How we got our Bible :

AN ANSWER TO QUESTIONS SUGGESTED BY THE RECENT REVISION.

BY

J. PATERSON SMYTH, B.D., LL.B.,

AUTHOR OF "HOW GOD INSPIRED THE BIBLE," "THE OLD DOCUMENTS AND THE NEW BIBLE," ETC.

NEW EDITION.
WITH ADDITIONAL ILLUSTRATIONS.

Multæ terricolis linguæ, cœlestibus una.

NEW YORK: JAMES POTT & CO.
LONDON: SAMUEL BAGSTER & SONS, LIMITED.

CONTENTS.

CHAPTER I.
SOURCES OF OUR BIBLE.

CHAPTER II.
ANCIENT MANUSCRIPTS.

CHAPTER III.
ANCIENT VERSIONS AND QUOTATIONS.

CHAPTER IV.
EARLY ENGLISH VERSIONS.

CHAPTER V.

WYCLIFFE'S VERSION.

CHAPTER VI.

TYNDALE'S VERSION.

CHAPTER VII.

THE BIBLE AFTER TYNDALE'S DAYS.

CHAPTER VIII.

THE REVISED VERSION.

PREFACE

TO THE TENTH EDITION.

SEVEN years ago, on the completion of the Revised Version of the Bible, this little book was written. Questions that must always be of interest to men were then brought into special prominence. Not only among the poorer classes, but among many more educated people as well, there was a vaguely puzzled half-suspicious feeling with regard to the new Bible attempting to supersede the venerable old version, which their fathers and forefathers for hundreds of years past had read as God's inspired message to the world. Men were surprised at finding some passages of the old Bible altered so as quite to change their meaning, and still more perhaps at noticing here and there verses entirely omitted, which they had always regarded as part of the inspired Word of God. And so the questions constantly arose when the New Version was talked of, "What fresh information has come to these Bible Revisers? By what right do men, 1800 years after the time of Our Lord, venture to meddle with the words of His revelation?" which easily led to still further questions as to the existence of the sacred originals of our present Scriptures, and the way in which these Scriptures have come down to us. It is a good thing that people should be roused by any cause to ask such questions, not merely because more attention will thereby be drawn to a Book on which such vital interests depend, but also and especially because he who seeks the answer to them, must indirectly learn, in pursuing his inquiry, what is of great importance to an intelligent appreciation of his Bible.

It is the smallest part of the gain of such an investigation that he should learn what Bible Revision really is, its continually recurring necessity, and the advantages that accrue from it if wisely and faithfully carried out.

He will also gain (what is of much value in these sceptical days) a view of the reception of the New Testament writings in the age soon after that of the apostles, in the lifetime of men whose fathers and grandfathers had been contemporaries of St. Paul and St. John. The inquiry will take him back to view the Scriptures of the second, and third, and fourth centuries, already translated into several different languages—to hear the testimony of a "great cloud of witnesses," the ablest scholars and deepest thinkers of those days bearing united testimony to these Scriptures as the production of the apostles and evangelists, regarding them with deepest reverence as the inspired Word of God, and earnestly devoting the best of their powers to the study and elucidation of them.

But perhaps the most important result from his inquiry will be the *sense of continuity* arising from the view, at various points, of the line of connection between the Apostolic Bible and our own—the conviction of the substantial identity of our Scriptures with those of the first century. One cannot help noticing what a haziness there is in many minds as to how this Bible of ours has come down to us, a haziness which in the writer's opinion is the fruitful parent of much unspoken doubt, or at least of that uneasy sense of "want of foundation" which, though most men are too indolent to trouble themselves about it, is often unconsciously undermining and weakening the power of their beliefs. The reason chiefly is that they cannot trace the *continuity* of the book from apostolic days to their own. They have just two points to fix upon, one the present existence of their English Bible—the other a dim hazy speck thousands of years ago, when, as they are told. "holy men of old spake as they were moved by the Holy Ghost," and between these two points is a great blank, where doubts about the Bible are easily developed, a blank which " Histories of the Bible," going back a few hundred years to Wycliffe's Version, do very little indeed to bridge over.

Such are some of the advantages that would result from a *thorough* study of this subject. Perhaps even by means of this little sketch, those results may in some small degree be gained to busy men and women who have neither the time nor opportunity for studying it more fully. At any rate the writer desires to keep this object before him while endeavouring to answer questions brought into prominence years ago by the appearance of a new version of the Bible, but which must remain of interest to Christian people as long as the Bible itself shall last.

HOW WE GOT OUR BIBLE.

CHAPTER I.

SOURCES OF OUR BIBLE.

§ 1. The Old Record Chest. § 2. Copyists' Errors. § 3. Necessity of Revision. § 4. Sources of Information open to Revisers. § 5. Special Reasons for Present Revision.

§ 1. LET us begin then by imagining before us the record chest of one of the early Christian churches,— say Jerusalem, or Rome, or Ephesus,—about 120 A.D., when sufficient time had elapsed since the completion of the New Testament writings to allow most of the larger churches to procure copies for themselves. In any one church, perhaps, we should not find very much, but if we collect together the documents of some of the leading churches we should have before us something of this sort :—

I. Some manuscripts of the Hebrew Old Testament books.

The reader will keep in mind that the Old Testament books were originally written in Hebrew, those of the New Testament in Greek.

II. A good many more of the Old Testament books translated into Greek for general use in the churches, Greek being the language most widely known at the time.

> This translation is called the Septuagint, or " Version of the
> *Seventy*," from an old tradition of its having been pre-
> pared by seventy learned Jews of Alexandria.[1] It was
> made at different times, beginning somewhere about 280
> B.C., and was the version commonly used by the Evange-
> lists and Apostles. This accounts for the slight difference
> we sometimes notice between the Old Testament and
> their quotations from it, our Old Testament being trans-
> lated direct from the Hebrew.

III. A few rolls of the Apocryphal Books, written by holy men in the Church, and valued for the prac-tical teaching they contained.

IV. Either the originals or direct copies of the Gospels and the Acts, the Epistles of SS. Paul and Peter and John, and the Book of the Revelation.

§ 2. Now let us remember clearly that as we look into that old record chest of nearly 1800 years ago, we have before us all the sources from which we get our Bible.

[1] One story is that King Ptolemy Lagi requested from the Jews at Jerusalem a Greek version of their Scriptures for his great Alexandrian Library ; that they sent seventy elders skilled in the Scriptures and in languages ; that the king separated them in different cells for their work, and that when they all appeared together before him with their versions, "God was glorified, for they all agreed exactly word for word." The truth probably is, that the version was made by Alexandrian Jews, whether for King Ptolemy or not we cannot tell.

And remember further that these writings were of course all manuscript, *i.e.*, written by the hand, and that copies when needed had each to be written out, letter by letter, at a great expense of time and trouble, and unfortunately, I must add, very often too at some expense of the original correctness. However careful the scribe might be, it was almost impossible, in copying a long and difficult manuscript, to prevent the occurrence of errors. Sometimes he would mistake one letter for another—sometimes, if having the manuscript read to him, he would confound two words of similar sound—sometimes after writing in the last word of a line, on looking up again his eye would catch the same word at the end of the next line, and he would go on from that, omitting the whole line between. Remarks and explanations, too, written in the margin might sometimes in transcribing get inserted in the text.

In these and various other ways errors might creep into the copy of his manuscript. These errors would be repeated by the man that afterwards copied from this, who would also sometimes add other errors of his own. So that it is evident, as copies increased, the errors would be likely to increase with them, and therefore, as a general rule,[1]

THE EARLIER ANY MANUSCRIPT, THE MORE LIKELY IT
   IS TO BE CORRECT.

---

[1] This is only a general rule. Of course it is quite possible for a manuscript A.D. 1500 to be copied *direct* from one of A.D. 300, and therefore to be more correct than some a thousand years older.

The reader may easily test this for himself by copying a dozen pages of a book, then hand on the copy
to a friend to re-copy, and let him pass on to another
what he has written, and so have the operation repeated
through six or eight different hands before comparing
the last copy with the original. It will be an interesting illustration of the danger of errors in copying.
Even in printed Bibles, whose proofs have been carefully examined and re-examined, these mistakes creep
in. To take two examples out of many :— An edition
published in 1653, reads 1 Cor. vi. 9, " Know ye not
that the unrighteous shall inherit the kingdom of
God ; " and the " Printer's Bible," much sought by
book collectors, puts the strange anachronism in King
David's mouth, " Printers have persecuted me without
a cause " (Ps. cxix. 161).

We know, of course, God might have miraculously
prevented scribes and compositors from making these
mistakes ; but it does not seem to be God's way anywhere to work miracles for us where our own careful
use of the abilities He has given would suffice for the
purpose.

§ 3. Although, owing to the special care exercised
in transcribing the Scriptures,[1] the errors would be in
most cases of comparatively trifling importance, yet it
is evident from what has been said about the growth

[1] As an interesting instance of the care exercised in transcribing important documents, Irenæus, Bishop of Lyons, in the second century,
thus writes in one of his own books : " Whosoever thou art who shalt
transcribe this book, I charge thee with an oath by our Lord Jesus

of copyists' errors, that in the course of the centuries before the invention of printing, Bible manuscripts might easily have grown very faulty indeed. Therefore the printed Bibles, taken hastily from these modern and probably corrupt manuscripts, would need a thorough revision, and this revision would need to be repeated again and again, as facilities increased, till the Scriptures were as nearly as possible as they left the inspired writers' hands.

But how is this revision to be accomplished? Of course, if the original writings had remained, it would be quite a simple operation, as a careful comparison with them would at any time discover whatever had need of correction. But, it is hardly necessary to say, the original writings have long since disappeared. Some of them, written on the common writing material of the day,—the papyrus paper referred to in 2 John, ver. 12,—very soon got worn out from use,[1] others were lost or destroyed in the early Christian persecutions. In any case they have totally disappeared.

How then is revision to be accomplished? In the

Christ, and by His glorious appearing, in which He cometh to judge the quick and dead, that thou carefully compare what thou hast transcribed, and correct it according to this copy whence thou hast transcribed it, and thou transcribe this oath in like manner, and place it in thy copy." Farther on I shall have to notice the solemn reverential care bestowed by the Hebrew scribes on copies of the Old Testament.

[1] Jerome tells of such a library in Cæsarea, already partly destroyed within a century after its formation, and of the endeavours of two presbyters to restore the manuscripts by copying them on parchment.

absence of these original manuscripts, what sources of information are open to Bible revisers?

§ 4. For answer let us turn from the ancient record chest, whose contents are now irrecoverably lost, and imagine beneath some oaken library roof a vast mass of manuscripts, piled up before us in THREE separate heaps,—manuscripts of very varied kind—stained and torn old parchments—books of faded purple, lettered with silver—beautifully designed ornamental pages—bundles of fine vellum, yellow with age, bright even yet with the gold and vermilion laid on by pious hands a thousand years since—in many shapes, in many colours, in many languages,—thousands of old Scripture writings reaching back for 1500 years.

This pile represents the great Biblical treasures stored up to-day in the various libraries of Europe—the Scriptures of all the ages almost from apostolic times. And here in this mass of old manuscripts is the material accessible to scholars for the purpose of Bible revision.

In these piles we shall find three different classes of writings. Here at the end those faded parchments, with the crowded square lettering, are *copies in the original languages* of the different Scriptures contained in the old record chest. These are known as Biblical "MANUSCRIPTS," for though all those early Scriptures are of course written by the hand, the name *manuscripts* has been by common consent of scholars appropriated to the *copies in the original tongue.*

But those farther on are evidently different in language, the writing, at least of the few whose pages are visible, being so very unlike the others. That open manuscript on the top, written all over in running lines and loops, is a Syriac translation, and all these are ANCIENT VERSIONS, *i.e.*, translations of the Bible into the languages of early Christendom, some of them representing the Scriptures of about fifty years after the apostles.

The contents of the third pile, though a good deal resembling the Biblical manuscripts in appearance, are not even books of the Scriptures at all, but WRITINGS OF THE EARLY CHRISTIAN FATHERS from the second to the fifth century. The use of these we shall see afterwards.

The science that deals with this mass of evidence is called "textual" criticism, a science which, though only in its infancy when our Authorised Version was issued, has reached in the present day a very high degree of perfection. Suppose then our revisers, men skilled in this study, are occupied on, say the Epistle to the Romans, desiring to present it as nearly as possible as it left the hands of St. Paul, how will they make use of this mass of evidence?

I. They will search for the *very oldest Greek manuscripts* in which the Epistle occurs, for, as we have already seen, the oldest are likely to be the most correct, and they will get *as many as possible* of them to compare them together for the eliminating any errors that may have crept in, for it is evident that if a number of copies are made of the same original, even should each of the copyists have erred, no two are likely to make exactly the same error, therefore a false reading in any one can often be corrected by comparison with the others.

II. Then they will examine the *ancient versions,* and see how the Epistle was read in Syriac and Latin and other ancient languages nearly 1700 years ago.

III. But what use can they make of the rest of the parchments—those writings of the early Christian Fathers? A very important use. They search these carefully for quotations from this Epistle. These early Fathers quoted Scripture so largely in their controversies that it has been said if all the other sources of the Bible were lost, we could recover the greater part of it from their writings. The most important of them lived in the second, third, and fourth centuries, and as they of course quote from the Scriptures in use in their time, it is like going back sixteen hundred years to ask men, How did your Scripture render this passage of St. Paul? Unfortunately their quotations seem often made from memory, which a good deal spoils the value of their testimony.

The sources of information, then, open to revisers may be briefly summed up as—

I. Manuscripts.   II. Versions.   III. Quotations.[1] Each of these will be treated of more fully in the following chapters.

[1] See Diagram facing the title-page.

SPECIMEN OF SYRIAC.

St. John I. 1–14.

PESHITO VERSION.

ܒ݉ܪܫܝܬ ܐܝܬܘܗܝ ܗܘܐ ܡܠܬܐ . ܘܗܘ ܡܠܬܐ
ܐܝܬܘܗܝ ܗܘܐ ܠܘܬ ܐܠܗܐ . ܘܐܠܗܐ ܐܝܬܘܗܝ
ܗܘܐ ܗܘ ܡܠܬܐ . ܗܢܐ ܐܝܬܘܗܝ ܗܘܐ ܒ݉ܪܫܝܬ
ܠܘܬ ܐܠܗܐ . ܟܠ ܒ݉ܐܝܕܗ ܗܘܐ . ܘܒܠܥܕܘܗܝ
ܐܦܠܐ ܚܕܐ ܗܘܬ݊ ܡܕܡ ܕ݉ܗܘܐ . ܒܗ ܚܝܐ ܗܘܐ .
ܘܚܝܐ ܐܝܬܝܗܘܢ ܢܘܗܪܐ ܕ݉ܒܢܝ̈ܢܫܐ .
ܘܗܘ ܢܘܗܪܐ ܒܚܫܘܟܐ ܡܢܗܪ : ܘܚܫܘܟܐ ܠܐ ܐܕܪܟܗ ⁘
ܗܘܐ ܒ݉ܪ݉ܢܫܐ ܕ݉ܐܫܬܕܪ ܡܢ ܐܠܗܐ : ܫܡܗ ܝܘܚܢܢ .
ܗܢܐ ܐܬܐ ܠܣܗܕܘܬܐ ܕ݉ܢܣܗܕ ܥܠ ܢܘܗܪܐ .
ܘܕ݉ܟܠܢܫ ܢܗܝܡܢ ܒ݉ܐܝܕܗ . ܠܐ ܗܘ ܗܘܐ
ܢܘܗܪܐ . ܐܠܐ ܕ݉ܢܣܗܕ ܥܠ ܢܘܗܪܐ . ܐܝܬܘܗܝ
ܗܘܐ ܓܝܪ ܢܘܗܪܐ ܕ݉ܫܪܪܐ : ܘܡܢܗܪ ܠܟܠܢܫ
ܕ݉ܐܬܐ ܠܥܠܡܐ . ܒܥܠܡܐ ܗܘܐ . ܘܥܠܡܐ
ܒ݉ܐܝܕܗ ܗܘܐ . ܘܥܠܡܐ ܠܐ ܝܕܥܗ . ܠܕܝܠܗ
ܐܬܐ . ܘܕܝܠܗ ܠܐ ܩܒܠܘܗܝ . ܐܝܠܝܢ ܕ݉ܝܢ
ܕ݉ܩܒܠܘܗܝ : ܝܗܒ ܠܗܘܢ ܫܘܠܛܢܐ ܕ݉ܒܢ̈ܝܐ
ܕ݉ܐܠܗܐ ܢܗܘܘܢ . ܠܐܝܠܝܢ ܕ݉ܡܗܝܡܢܝܢ ܒ݉ܫܡܗ .
ܐܝܠܝܢ ܕܠܘ ܡܢ ܕ݉ܡܐ . ܘܠܐ ܡܢ ܨܒܝܢܐ ܕ݉ܒܣܪܐ .
ܘܠܐ ܡܢ ܨܒܝܢܐ ܕ݉ܓܒܪܐ ܐܠܐ ܡܢ ܐܠܗܐ ܐܬܝܠܕܘ .
ܘܡܠܬܐ ܒܣܪܐ ܗܘܐ ܘܐܓܢ ܒܢ . ܘܚܙܝܢ
ܫܘܒܚܗ . ܫܘܒܚܐ ܐܝܟ ܕ݉ܝܚܝܕܝܐ ܕ݉ܡܢ ܐܒܐ :
ܕ݉ܡܠܐ ܛܝܒܘܬܐ ܘܩܘܫܬܐ ⁘

§ 5. Now the reason that so much has been said about the possible errors of copyists and our means of correcting them is that we may be in a position to understand clearly the reason of the recent Bible revision and what grounds the revisers had for altering anything.

First, then, we have access to a great many more and older manuscripts and versions and quotations than the men who prepared the Authorised Version had ever heard of.

Besides, our scholars understand those ancient languages and the science of textual criticism far better than did the scholars of King James' time.

And to these we may add a third reason, one which would always make Bible revision a necessity, even if there were no advances in scholarship or manuscript discoveries—I mean the changes owing to the natural growth of language. More than 200 words in the Authorised Version have thus changed their meaning, *e.g.*, carriages, comfort, common, conversation, damnation, let, malice, mortify, prevent, master, quick; also phrases such as, to take thought, &c., and the change often affects the meaning of important passages.

Therefore we are able to detect faults even in our almost perfect Authorised Version—mistakes here and there which scholars have known of for some time past; verses where the rendering needed to be improved, and in a few instances passages whose right to stand in the Bible at all was very doubtful. In such cases

I need hardly say that no amount of sentiment about our grand old Bible should prevent our making the corrections required.

In the following chapters we shall go through in more detail this mass of ancient manuscript evidence accessible to our revisers, and examine some of the oldest and most important writings, that we may the better understand what facilities scholars have at the present day for undertaking a Bible revision.

CHAPTER II.

ANCIENT MANUSCRIPTS.

The Oldest Bibles in the World. § 1. The Vatican Manuscript. § 2. The Sinaitic Manuscript. § 3. The Alexandrian. § 4. Palimpsests. § 5. Cursive Manuscripts. § 6. Old Testament Revision.

LET us still keep imaged before our minds the triple pile of Biblical writings to be examined.

We come first to the MANUSCRIPTS, the *copies* [1] of the Scripture in the original tongues. Of the Greek there is quite a large number—more than 1500—before us, and from the difference in their condition and general appearance one is inclined to suspect that they must vary a good deal in age, and therefore probably in value. The question of determining the age of a manuscript is a very intricate one; but it should make our inspection of these the more interesting if I briefly state a few easy marks to guide us :—

The form of the letters is the chief guide. The oldest and therefore most valuable are written in capital

---

[1] The reader should keep this distinction clearly before him to prevent confusion. MANUSCRIPTS = copies in the original tongue. VERSIONS = translations into other tongues.

letters, and without any division between the words,
as if we should write

NOWWHENJSWASBORNINBETHLEHEMOFJ.

These are called *uncial* manuscripts. The modern
are written in a running hand like our writing, and
are therefore called *cursive*. (It will be useful to
remember these names, as they frequently occur in
Bible commentaries, and in criticisms of the Revised
Version.)

Then again, initial letters, miniatures, and in general any ornamentation of manuscripts, marks them as
of comparatively late date.

Far the greater number of the manuscripts before
us are written in the cursive hand, many of them
beautifully illuminated and ornamented with exquisite
miniatures and initials. But we turn at once from
these to their less attractive companions, those few
faded, worn parchments with the old uncial letters.
Notice especially those three at the end bound in square
book form; they are plain, faded-looking documents,
with little about them to attract attention, but these
three manuscripts are among the greatest treasures the
Christian Church possesses—the oldest copies of the
Bible in the world! They are named respectively the
Vatican, Sinaitic, and Alexandrian Manuscripts. They
have been largely used in the recent Bible Revision,
*but they were not any of them accessible to those who
prepared the Authorised Version in* 1611.

These three oldest manuscripts are curiously enough

Facing page 21.]

THE SINAITIC MANUSCRIPT.

Photographed from one of the scraps found by Dr. Tischendorf in the Old Basket at Mount Sinai (see p. 24).

in possession of the three great branches of the Christian Church. The ALEXANDRIAN (called for shortness *Codex* A) belongs to Protestant England, and is kept in the manuscript room of the British Museum; the VATICAN (*Codex* B) is in the Vatican Library at Rome; and the SINAITIC (*Codex* Aleph), which has only lately been discovered, is one of the treasures of the Greek Church at St. Petersburg.

These manuscripts show us the Bible as it existed soon after the apostolic days. There has been a good deal of discussion about their age, which need not be entered on here; but we shall not be far from the truth if we say roundly that they range from about 300 to 450 A.D. Therefore the oldest is about as distant in time from the original inspired writings as the Revised is from the Authorised Version. All the Greek manuscripts before this time seem to have perished in the terrible persecutions which were directed not only against the Christians themselves, but also and with special force against their sacred writings.

§ I. THE VATICAN MANUSCRIPT. Each of these three manuscripts has its history. The most ancient, it is generally agreed, is the Vatican Manuscript, which has lain at least four or five hundred years in the Vatican Library at Rome. One is much inclined to grudge the Roman Church the possession of this our most valuable manuscript; for the papal authorities have been very jealous guardians, and most persons capable of examining it aright have been refused access to it.

Dr. Tregelles, one of our most eminent students of textual criticism, made an attempt; but he says they would not let him open the volume without searching his pockets, and depriving him of pens and ink and paper; the two priests told off to watch him would try to distract his attention if he seemed too intent on any passage, and if he studied any part of it too long they would snatch away the book. However, it has of late years become easily accessible through the excellent fac-similes made by order of Pope Pius IX., which may be seen in our chief public libraries.

Here is the manuscript itself, over 700 leaves of the finest vellum, about a foot square, bound together in book form. You will see that it is not quite perfect, having lost Gen. i.–xlvi., as well as Psalms cv.–cxxxvii., and all after Heb. ix. 14 of the New Testament. The original writing must have been beautifully delicate and finely formed. There are only a few words left here and there by which to judge of this; for from one end to the other, the whole manuscript has been travelled over by the pen of some meddlesome scribe of about the tenth century. Probably he was afraid of the precious writing fading out if it were not thus inked over; but if so his fears were quite groundless, for here are some of the words which he passed over (considering them incorrect) remaining still perfectly clear and legible after the lapse of 1500 years. Each page contains three columns, and the writing, you see, is in capital letters, without any division between the words. This makes it less easy to read, but of course it was done to save space at a time when writing material was very expensive.

To carry this saving further, words are written smaller and more crowded as they approach the end of a line, and for the same reason was adopted the plan of contracted words, which has often been the cause of manuscript errors. First, they cut off the final M's and N's at the end of a word, marking the omission by a line across the top, as if we should write LONDŌ for London; then they proceeded to the dropping of final syllables, and from that to the shortening of frequently recurring words, like the name Jesus or God. We might fairly represent these peculiarities (which are common to all the early manuscripts) by writing thus in English (Titus ii. 11, 12):

FORTHEGRACEOFGŌDBRINGING
SALVATIONHATHAPPEARED
TOALLM̄NTEACHINGUSTHATDEN
YINGUNGODLINESSANDWOR
LDLYLUSTWESHOULDLIVESOB
ERLYANDGODLYINTHISPRESENT
EVILWORLDLOOKINGFORTHAT

One remark more before we lay it aside. You will notice in the Revised New Testament the passage at the end of St. Mark's Gospel printed in as in some degree doubtful, and a notice in the margin that "the two oldest Greek manuscripts omit these verses." Now this and the Sinaitic are the two manuscripts referred to, and if we turn to the place you will see that this one, while omitting the passage, curiously enough leaves a blank space for it on the page, showing that the scribe knew of its existence, but was undecided whether he should put it in or not.

§ 2. THE SINAITIC MANUSCRIPT. There is no need of describing this celebrated manuscript, which on the whole you see very much resembles the other; but the story of its discovery about forty years ago is full of interest. It is called the Sinaitic Manuscript from the place where it was found by the great German scholar, Dr. Tischendorf. His whole life was given up to the discovery and study of ancient manuscripts of the Bible, and he travelled all over the East, searching every old library he could get into for the purpose; but it was quite unexpectedly in St. Catharine's Convent, at the foot of Mount Sinai, that he discovered this the "pearl of all his researches," as he calls it.

In visiting the library of the convent in the month of May 1844, he perceived in the middle of the great hall a basket full of old parchments, and the librarian told him that two heaps of similar old documents had already been used for the fires. What was his surprise to find in the basket a number of sheets of a copy of the Septuagint (Greek) Old Testament, the most ancient-looking manuscript that he had ever seen. The authorities of the convent allowed him to take away about forty sheets, as they were only intended for the fire; but he displayed so much satisfaction with his gift that the suspicion of the monks was aroused as to the value of the manuscript, and they refused to give him any more.

He returned to Germany, and with his precious sheets made a great sensation in the literary world. But he took very good care not to tell where he had got them, as he still had hopes of securing the remainder ; and he soon had reason to congratulate himself on his caution, for the English Government at once sent out a scholar to buy up any valuable Greek manuscripts he could lay hands on, and poor Dr. Tischendorf was very uneasy lest the Englishman should stumble upon the old basket on Mount Sinai. You may judge of his relief when he saw the Englishman's report soon after, telling of his failure ; " for," said he, " after the visit of such a critic as Dr. Tischendorf, I could not, of course, expect any success." The doctor seems quite to enjoy the telling this part of the story.

He tried next, by means of an influential friend at the court of Egypt, to procure the rest of the manuscript, but without success. " The monks of the convent," wrote his friend, " have since your departure learned the value of the parchments, and now they will not part with them at any price." So he paid another visit to Mount Sinai, but could only find one sheet, containing eleven lines of the book of Genesis, which showed him that the manuscript originally contained the entire Old Testament.

To shorten the story, I must pass over fifteen years, during which time he had enlisted the sympathy of the Emperor of Russia, and in 1859 we find him again at the convent with a commission from the Emperor himself. However, he found very little of any value, and had made his arrangements to leave without accomplishing his mission, when a quite unexpected event brought about all that he wished for. The very evening before he was to leave he was walking in the grounds with the steward of the convent, and as they returned the monk asked him into his cell to take some refreshment. Scarcely had they entered the cell, when, resuming his former conversation, the monk said : " I too have read a copy of that Septuagint." And so saying he took down a bulky bundle, wrapped in red cloth, and laid it on the table. Tischendorf opened the parcel, and to his great surprise found not only those very fragments that he had seen fifteen years before, but also other parts of the Old Testament, the New Testament complete, and some of the Apocryphal Books.

Full of joy, which this time he had the self-command to conceal, he asked in a careless way for permission to look over it in his bedroom. " And there by myself," he says, " I gave way to my transports of joy. I knew that I held in my hand one of the most precious Biblical treasures in existence, a document whose age and importance exceeded that of any I had ever seen after twenty years' study of the subject."

At length, through the Emperor's influence, he succeeded in obtaining the precious manuscript, which is now stored up in the Library of St. Petersburg, the greatest treasure which the Eastern Church possesses. Strange that after all the vicissitudes of fifteen centuries it should at length be restored to the world only twenty-five years since! It is now easily accessible to scholars through its fac-similes in all our great libraries. See photograph at p. 21.

§ 3. THE ALEXANDRIAN MANUSCRIPT (Codex A). This youngest of our three great manuscripts has special interest for us, being in the custody of England, and preserved with our great national treasures in the British Museum. It was presented to Charles I. by Cyril Lucar, Patriarch of Constantinople, A.D. 1628, and therefore arrived in England seventeen years too late to be of use in preparing our Authorised Version. Notice the Arabic inscription on the first sheet, stating that it was written "by the hand of Thekla the Martyr."

Only ten leaves are missing from the Old Testament part, but the New Testament is much more defective, having lost twenty-five leaves from the beginning of St. Matthew, two from St. John, and three from Corinthians. It is written, you see, two columns on a page, the Vatican and Sinaitic having respectively three and four. The original can be seen at the British Museum, but copies which exactly represent it are, like those of the other two, kept in our chief public libraries.

§ 4. Here is the Codex of Ephraem, a very curious manuscript, all stained and soiled, and seemingly of little value, as it is written in quite a modern hand. It requires a closer examination to notice under that straggling handwriting the faint, faded lines of old uncial letters. This is what is called a Palimpsest or Rescript Manuscript, *i.e.*, one that has had its original contents rubbed out to make room for some other writing. We noticed already contractions, &c., adopted to save parchment at a time when it was very expensive. For the same purpose scribes sometimes used old parchments that had been written on before, and, by carefully scraping and pumicing out the old letters, made the skin tolerably fit for use again.

It need hardly be said that in many cases the writing thus blotted out was of far greater value than that which replaced it, and especially is it so in this case, where an ancient and valuable copy of the Scriptures was in the twelfth century coolly scrubbed out to make room for some theological discourses of Ephraem, an old Syrian Father.

The old writing, however, had not been so thoroughly rubbed but that some dim traces remained, which drew attention to the manuscript about 200 years since. It was very difficult to decipher the old hand till some chemical preparation applied in 1834 revived a good part of it, though it very much stained and defaced the vellum. The MS. was then found to contain a considerable portion of both Old and New Testaments, and it is considered almost if not quite as old as the Alexandrian. It belongs to the Royal Library at Paris.

Here is another of those interesting Palimpsest manuscripts, in possession of Trinity College, Dublin, and lying beside it a later one, the Codex Zacynthus

Photographed from the DUBLIN UNIVERSITY PALIMPSEST,
Codex " Z."

Notice under the writing the faintly appearing letters of the Old Bible
that had been rubbed out.

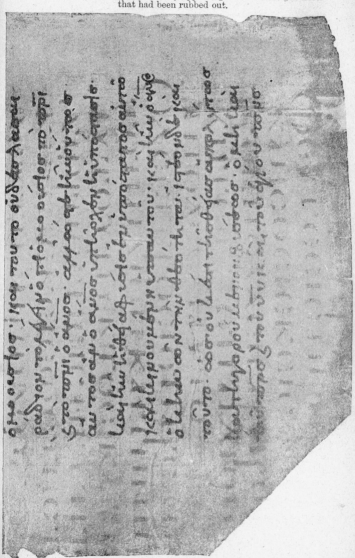

from the Library of the British and Foreign Bible Society.

§ 5. All that we have examined up to this date are of uncial type, which, as we have seen, is a mark of their antiquity. Of these Uncials we have altogether about a hundred.

Of the more modern manuscripts, in the cursive or running hand, there are more than 1500 accessible to scholars. It has been already remarked that it is quite possible for a comparatively modern manuscript to possess a high value, as, for example, suppose a scribe of the fifteenth century had copied in running hand direct from the " Vatican." For this and other reasons some of our Cursives are very important evidence. There is one, for instance, the " Queen of the Cursives," as it is called, which, for its valuable readings, ranks above many a far older Uncial, and there are four others, quite modern in date (twelfth to fourteenth centuries), which have been shown by Professor Abbott and the late Professor Ferrar, of Trinity College, Dublin,[1] to be transcribed from one and the same ancient manuscript, which was probably little later than our Alexandrian Codex.

If we remember that ten or twelve manuscripts, and these generally modern, are all we have for ascertaining the text of most classical authors, it will help us to understand what an enormous mass of evidence there is available for the purpose of Scripture revision.

[1] "Collation of Four Important Manuscripts," by W. H. Ferrar, F.T.C.D., edited by T. K. Abbott, F.T.C.D. Dublin, 1877.

§ 6. The Hebrew manuscripts of the Old Testament need occupy little time, the earliest we possess dating no earlier than about the tenth century. The lack of early manuscripts here is, however, of less importance. As far as we can learn there seems to have been a gradual rough sort of revision of the Palestine manuscripts continually going on almost from the days of Ezra. About a thousand years ago this process of Hebrew Manuscript Revision came to an end, and thus at that early date the Hebrew Old Testament was made as nearly correct as the best scholarship of the Jewish academies could make it, after which the older manuscripts gradually disappeared.

The existing Hebrew manuscripts, then, though not very old, are of great authority, and all the more so owing to the reverence of Jewish scribes for the Word of God, and the consequent carefulness of their transcription. So scrupulous were they that even if a manifest error were in the copy they transcribed from, they would not meddle with it in the text, but would write in the margin what the true reading should be; if they found one letter larger than another, or a word running beyond the line, or any other mere irregularity, they would copy it exactly as it stood. They recorded how many verses in each book, and the middle verse of each, and how many verses began with particular letters, &c., &c. Such exactness, of course, very much lessened the danger of erroneous copying, and makes our Hebrew Scriptures far more trustworthy than they could otherwise be.

The reason then that there are so few changes in the Revised Old Testament, as compared with the New, is that we have less need as well as less means of making any corrections.[1] In fact, the chief grounds for undertaking Old Testament revision are the increased knowledge of Hebrew and of textual criticism, together with the changes through natural growth of the English language itself. We may add also, for their united evidence is very important, the more thorough study in late years of the Septuagint and the Targums, together with the Vulgate and other ancient versions, to be described in the next chapter.

[1] It is no reflection on the Old Testament Revisers to suggest also that they could scarcely avoid being influenced in some degree by the strong feeling exhibited against the many changes in the New Testament portion.

CHAPTER III.

ANCIENT VERSIONS AND QUOTATIONS.

§ 1. Various Early Versions. § 2. An ancient "Revised Bible." § 3. How Revision was regarded fifteen centuries ago. § 4. Advantage of this investigation. § 5. Quotations from Ancient Fathers.

§ 1. WE are to examine now our second pile—the ANCIENT VERSIONS, *i.e.*, the translations of the Bible into the languages of early Christendom long before the oldest of our present Greek manuscripts were written. These were the Bibles used by men, some of whose parents might easily have seen the apostles themselves, and therefore it is evident that, even though only translations, they must often be of great value in determining the original text.

There are the old Syriac Scriptures, which were probably in use about fifty years after the New Testament was written, a Version representing very nearly the language of the people among whom our Lord moved. Those discoloured parchments beside them are Egyptian, Ethiopic, and Armenian Versions, which would be more useful if our scholars understood these languages better; and the beautiful silver-lettered book,

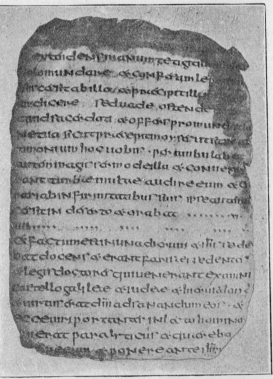

with its leaves of purple parchment, is the Version of Ulfilas, bishop of the fierce Gothic tribes about A.D. 350.[1] Here are the old Latin, which, with the Syriac, are the earliest of all our Versions, and the most valuable for the purpose of textual criticism.

But what is this Version piled up in such enormous numbers, far exceeding that of all the others put together, some of its copies, too, ornamented with exquisite beauty ?

§ 2. It is a Version which just now should possess very special interest for English readers—St. Jerome's Latin Vulgate, the great "Revised Bible" of the ancient Western Church. This is its story.

Towards the end of the fourth century, so many errors had crept into the old Latin Versions, that the Latin-speaking churches were in danger of losing the pure Scripture of the apostolic days. Just at this crisis, when scholars were keenly feeling the need of a revision, there returned to Rome from his Bethlehem hermitage one of the greatest scholars and holiest men of the day, Eusebius Hieronymus, better known to us as St. Jerome, and his high reputation pointed him out at once as the man to undertake this important task. Damasus, bishop of Rome, applied to him for that purpose, and Jerome undertook the revision, though he was deeply sensible of the prejudice which his work would arouse among those who, he says,

---

[1] Gibbon says : " He prudently suppressed the four books of Kings, as they might tend to irritate the fierce spirit of the barbarians."

"thought that ignorance was holiness." His revision of the New Testament was completed in 385, and the Old Testament he afterwards translated direct from the original Hebrew, a task which probably no other scholar of the time would have been capable of. We shall better understand the value of his work if we remember that it is almost as old as the earliest of our present Greek manuscripts, and since Jerome of course used the oldest manuscripts to be had in his day, his authorities would have probably extended back to the days of the apostles.

No other work has ever had such an influence on the history of the Bible. For more than a thousand years it was the parent of every version of the Scriptures [1] in Western Europe, and even now, when the Greek and Hebrew manuscripts are so easily accessible, the Rhemish and Douay Testaments are translations direct from the Vulgate, and its influence is quite perceptible even on our own Authorised Version.

§ 3. How do you think the good people of the fourth century thanked St. Jerome for his wonderful Bible? Remembering the prejudice which our Revised New Testament excited only a few years ago, it is interesting to recall the story how the Revision of the old monk of Bethlehem was received.

It was called revolutionary and heretical; it was pronounced subversive of all faith in Holy Scriptures; it was said to be an impious altering of the Inspired

[1] See Diagram facing the title-page.

Word of God.   In fact, for centuries after, everything
was said against it that ignorant bigotry could suggest
to bring it into disrepute.   The Christians of that day
had their old Bible, which they venerated highly and
believed to be quite correct, and probably the sound of
its sentences was as musical in their ears, who could
associate them with the holiest moments of their lives,
as that of our beautiful old version is in ours.

But St. Jerome fought his battle, perhaps with more
temper than was necessary,[1] insisting that no amount
of sentiment could be a plea for a faulty Bible, and
that the most venerable translation must give way if
found to disagree with the original text.

It is instructive to us to see how completely the tide
had turned at the time of the Council of Trent, a thousand years later.   Men had then got as attached to the
version of St. Jerome as those of the fourth century
had been to its predecessors.   In fact, they seem almost
to have forgotten that it was only a translation.   It is
the version of the Church, they said, and in her own
language ; " Why should it yield to Greek and Hebrew

[1] Thus, writing to Marcella, he mentions certain poor creatures
(homunculos), who studiously calumniate him for his correcting words
in the Gospels.   "I could afford to despise them," he says, "if I stood
upon my rights ; for a lyre is played in vain to an ass.   If they do not
like the water from the pure fountain-head, let them drink of the
muddy streams ; " and again, at the close of the letter, he returns to
the attack of those "bipedes asellos" (two-legged donkeys).   " Let
them read, ' *Rejoicing in hope, serving the time ;*' let *us* read, ' Rejoicing
in hope, serving the Lord ;*' let *them* consider that an accusation should
not under any circumstances be received against an elder ; let *us* read,
' Against an elder receive not an accusation ; but before two or three
witnesses,' " &c. (Ep. 28).

manuscripts, which have been for all these hundreds of years in the hands of Jewish unbelievers and Greek schismatics?" Well, how did they act? They decreed in council that the old Vulgate should be considered correct, and to this day, with all the progress in textual research, their Church has refused to advance any farther,

> "Resting, amid the rush of progression,
> Like a frozen ship on a frozen sea."

An amusing exhibition of their feeling at the time is a passage in the preface to the Complutensian Polyglot Bible, where the Hebrew and the Greek and the Latin Vulgate were printed in parallel columns side by side, the venerable old Vulgate being in the middle, which the editors with grim humour compared to the position of our Lord between the two thieves at the crucifixion! Of course they did not mean any slight to the original Scriptures, but their prejudice led them to suspect, or to fancy they had a right to suspect, that the Jews and Greeks might have corrupted the manuscript copies.

§ 4. This glance at the Ancient Versions will be sufficient for our purpose. There is a large number now accessible to scholars, and every year the study of them is increasing. In passing, I would point to this part of our subject to illustrate what was said in the introduction of the advantage indirectly resulting from the investigation of questions suggested by our

New Revision. For here we find that at a time when some sceptical writers would have us believe our New Testament books were scarcely written, they had been translated and copied and re-copied in the languages of early Christendom; commentaries and harmonies of the Gospels had been written; a list of the books had been prepared (of which we have still a portion called the Muratorian Fragment), and they were regarded in all arguments between Christians of the time as referees having divine authority. All this will be seen still more clearly after we have briefly glanced at the third source of information open to revisers :—

§ 5. THE QUOTATIONS IN EARLY CHRISTIAN WRITERS. The quantity of these writings is great, but they have been up to this time very imperfectly examined. In spite of the disadvantages of the quotations being often fragmentary, and sometimes—as will be seen in the examples—made loosely from memory, they are yet of great value in determining the text of ancient Bibles, some of them going back to the days of the original New Testament writings. Let us turn over a few of them at random, taking the earliest in preference.

(a.) Here is the Epistle of Barnabas, which Dr. Tischendorf found bound up with his Sinaitic Manuscript. It is supposed, though without good reason, to have been written by St. Paul's companion; but certainly it is not much later than his date. Notice these expressions: Beware, therefore, lest it come upon us as it is written, "There be many called but few chosen;" again, "Give to him that asketh thee." And farther on he says, "that Christ chose as His apostles men who were sinners, because He came not to call the righteous, but sinners to repentance."

(b.) This next is an Epistle by Clement, one of the early bishops of Rome, whom ancient writers unhesitatingly assert to be the Clement mentioned by St. Paul in Phil. iv. 3. This letter is a very valuable one, and Irenæus, who was bishop of Lyons a little later, says of it, "It was written by Clement, who had seen the blessed apostles and conversed with them, who had the preaching of the blessed apostles still sounding in his ears and their tradition before his eyes." The epistle was addressed to the Church of Corinth, and Dionysius, bishop of Corinth about 170 A.D., bears witness "that it had been wont to be read in his church from ancient times." Here are a few expressions found in it: "Remembering the words of the Lord Jesus which He spake, teaching us gentleness and long-suffering; for He said, 'Be merciful, that ye may obtain mercy; forgive, that it may be forgiven unto you; as ye give it shall be given unto you; as ye judge ye shall be judged; with what measure ye mete, it shall be measured to you.'"

And again, "Remember the words of the Lord Jesus, how He said, 'Woe to the man by whom offences come; it were better for him that he had not been born than that he should offend one of My elect. It were better for him that a millstone should be tied about his neck, and that he should be drowned in the depths of the sea, than that he should offend one of My little ones.'"

(*c.*) Of about the same date is this book, the Shepherd of Hermas, by some conjectured to be the Hermas of Rom. xvi. 14. Here we have reference to the confessing and denying of Christ, the parable of the seed sown, the expression, "He that putteth away his wife and marrieth another, committeth adultery," &c. &c.

(*d.*) St. Ignatius became bishop of Antioch about forty years after the Ascension. Here are a few quotations from him : "Christ was baptized of John, that all righteousness might be fulfilled in Him." "Be ye wise as serpents in all things, and harmless as a dove." "The Spirit is from God, for it knows whence it cometh and whither it goeth."

(*e.*) The martyr Polycarp was a disciple of St. John, and is thus spoken of by Irenæus, bishop of Lyons, who in his youth had seen him : "I can tell the place in which the blessed Polycarp sat and taught, and his going out and coming in, and the manner of his life, and how he related his conversations with John and others who had seen the Lord, all which Polycarp related agreeably to the Scriptures." Of this old martyr we have an epistle remaining, and though it is a very short one, it contains nearly forty clear allusions to the New Testament books, some of which are valuable for critical purposes.

(*f.*) Those old parchments lying beside Polycarp's Epistle, are the "Apologies," by Justin Martyr, and his

"Dialogue with Trypho," written about the year 150. They contain very interesting quotations, though unfortunately they seem often quoted from memory, and therefore lose much of their value. This is only what we might expect. "When we think it strange," says Dr. Salmon in a recent book,[1] "that an ancient father of Justin's date should not quote with perfect accuracy, we forget that in those days, when manuscripts were scarce and concordances did not exist, the process of finding a passage in a manuscript (written possibly with no spaces between the words) was not performed with quite as much ease as an English clergyman writing his sermon, with a Bible and Concordance by his side, can turn up any text he wishes to refer to, and yet we should be sorry to vouch for the verbal accuracy of all the Scripture citations we hear in sermons at the present day."

The following are a few of Justin's quotations:—
'I gave you power to tread on serpents and scorpions, and venomous beasts, and on all the power of the enemy." "Give to him that asketh, and from him that would borrow turn not away; for if ye lend to them of whom ye hope to receive, what new thing do ye? Even the publicans do this. Lay not up for yourselves treasures upon earth, where moth and rust doth corrupt, and where robbers break through; but lay up for yourselves treasure in heaven, where neither môth nor rust doth corrupt." "For what is a man profited if he shall gain the whole world and lose his own soul,

[1] "Introd. New Testament," p. 82.

or what shall a man give in exchange for it?" And again, "Be ye kind and merciful, as your Father also is kind and merciful, and maketh His sun to rise on sinners, and the righteous and the wicked. Take no thought what ye shall eat or what ye shall put on; are ye not better than the birds and the beasts? and God feedeth them. Take no thought, therefore, what ye shall eat or what ye shall put on, for your heavenly Father knoweth that ye have need of these things. But seek ye the kingdom of heaven, and all these things shall be added unto you. For where his treasure is, there is the mind of man."

On account of the double object in view, I have selected only writers of the second century to illustrate the use of the "Quotations." More important for purposes of criticism, though later in date, are those thick manuscripts further on, the works of Origen and Clement of Alexandria early in the third century, and in the fourth Basil, and Augustine, and Jerome the great reviser, and many others, whose writings in large quantity are available for criticism of the Bible.

CHAPTER IV.

EARLY ENGLISH VERSIONS.

§ 1. The Bible Poet. § 2. Eadhelm and Egbert. § 3. The Monk of Yarrow. § 4. A Royal Translator. § 5. Curious Expressions.

THUS we have seen the form in which the Scriptures existed in the age soon after that of the apostles, and found the threefold line of evidence available at the present day for the purpose of Bible Revision—(1.) Greek and Hebrew manuscripts; (2.) Ancient Versions; and (3.) Quotations from the then existing Scriptures in the works of early Christian writers.

And now that we are to trace the connection of these with our present English Bible, it becomes necessary for our purpose to ask, with the triple pile of parchments before us, how much of this material was accessible a thousand years ago, when the history of our English Bible begins. For it is evident that the value of a Scripture version at any period depends on the value of the old manuscript material accessible, and the ability of the men of that day to use it.

For answer we take from the centre pile those few faded worn-looking copies, portions of the Vulgate and older Latin versions, and place them on one side.[1] Those are the Scriptures which have come down to us from the monasteries of ancient England, and as we compare side by side this handful of old parchments with the great mass of writings from which it has been drawn, we are comparing together the sources of the earliest and latest English Versions—of the Anglo-Saxon Scriptures of a thousand years since, and the Revised Bible which is in our hands to-day.[2] The growth of the English Bible, which took place in the meantime, we are now briefly to trace.[3]

[1] There were also many works of the early Christian Fathers, but as no one then thought of using them for purposes of textual criticism, we need not take them into account.

[2] On page facing the title I have tried to show by a diagram the gradual increase in the sources of our English Bible.

[3] Here comes a temptation to an Irish writer. Is he bound to start from the seventh century, when the earliest known translations from these manuscripts were made? May he not go back a little further, and let rise the historic memories called up by those manuscripts themselves? May he not indulge a little in the "Irish pride of better days" (the only source of pride to poor Ireland in the present), and picture the noble libraries of Durrow and Armagh, to which England probably owes her earliest Scriptures—when St. Columb carried his manuscripts to lonely Iona in the days of the glory of the Irish Church, when Ireland was the light of the Western World, and Irishmen went forth from the "Island of Saints" to evangelise the heathen English?

At any rate it seems worth spending a few sentences to point out that not from Rome, but from the ancient Irish Church, did England chiefly derive her Christianity, and probably her earliest Scriptures. What seems best remembered in connection with the question, is the famous scene of Gregory in the slave-market at Rome, admiring the beautiful English children—"not Angles, but angels," said he, "if they were only Christians"—and the consequent sending of the Abbot Augustine to England with a band of Christian missionaries. It needs to be

§ 1. Though England had no complete Bible before Wycliffe's days, attempts were made from very early times to present the Scriptures in the language of the people, and the story of these ancient translations from the Latin manuscripts before us, forms certainly one of the most interesting though not most important portions of the history of the English Bible.

It is now 1200 years since, on a winter night, a poor Saxon cowherd lay asleep in a stable of the famous Abbey of Whitby. Grieved and dispirited, he had come in from the feast where his masters, and some even of his companions, during the amusements of the night, had engaged in the easy, alliterative rhyming of those simple early days. But Cædmon could make no song,[1] and his soul was very sad. Suddenly, as he lay,

pointed out that, according to our best historians, this Roman mission soon lost its early ardour, penetrating little further than Kent, where it originally landed, and that the conversion of England, which had become completely pagan under Saxon rule, was for the most part left to the missionaries of the Irish Church. From St. Columb's monastery at Iona the Irish preachers came, and travelled over the greater part of the country. Aidan, their leader, went through the wilds of Yorkshire and Northumbria, with King Oswald as his interpreter, a former student of Iona—while Chad and Boisil led their little bands of missionaries through the centre of the heathen land, returning at stated periods to Lindisfarne, where Aidan had fixed his episcopal see. And not England only owes a debt to the Irish Church. As far off as the Apennines and the Alps the traces of her enthusiastic missionaries are found, and "for a time it seemed as if the course of the world's history was to be changed, as if the older Celtic race, that Roman and German had swept before them, had turned to the moral conquest of their conquerors, as if Celtic and not Latin Christianity was to mould the destinies of the churches of the West."

[1] "Being at the feast, when all agreed for glee sake to sing in turn, he no sooner saw the harp come towards him, than he rose from the board and returned homewards."—*Account of Cædmon in Bede's Eccl. Hist.*

it seemed to him that a heavenly glory lighted up his stable, and in the midst of the glory One appeared who had been cradled in a manger six hundred years before.

" Sing, Cædmon," He said, " sing some song to me."

" I cannot sing," was the sorrowful reply, " for this cause it is that I came hither."

" Yet," said He who stood before him, " yet shalt thou sing to me."

" What shall I sing ? "

" The beginning of created things."

And as he listened, a divine power seemed to come on him, and words that he had never heard before rose up before his mind.[1] And so the vision passed away. But the power remained with Cædmon, and in the morning the Saxon cowherd went forth from the cattle-stalls transformed into a mighty poet !

Hilda the abbess heard the wondrous tale, and from one of those Latin manuscripts she translated to him a story of the Scriptures. Next day it was reproduced in a beautiful poem, followed by another and another as the spirit of the poet grew powerful within him. Entranced, the abbess and the brethren heard, and they acknowledged the " grace that had

---

[1] The words that came to the sleeper's mind are recorded by King Alfred. They begin :—

> " Now must we praise
> the grandeur of Heaven's kingdom ;
> the Creator's might,
> and his mind's thought ;
> glorious father of men,
> The Lord the Eternal,
> who formed the beginning," &c. &c.

been conferred on him by the Lord." They bade him lay aside his secular habit and enter the monastic life, and from that day forward the Whitby cowherd devoted himself with enthusiasm to the task that had been set him in the vision. "Others after him strove to compose religious poems, but none could vie with him, for he learnt not the art of poetry from men, neither of men, but of God." In earnest passionate words, which yet remain, he sung for the simple people "of the creation of the world, of the origin of man, and of all the history of Israel; of the Incarnation, and Passion, and Resurrection of Christ, and His Ascension; of the terror of future judgment, the horror of hell pains, and the joys of the kingdom of heaven." [1]

Though his work has of course no right to rank among Bible translations, being merely an attempt to sing for the ignorant people the substance of the inspired story, yet we venture to give a brief extract, translated into modern English, telling of the appearance of Christ to His disciples after the resurrection :—

> " What time the Lord God
> from death arose
> so strongly was no
> Satan armed
> though he were with iron
> all girt round

[1] "Some account of Cædmon from Bede's Eccl. Hist., translated into Anglo-Saxon by King Alfred."—*Published by the Society of Antiquaries, London.*

that might that great
force resist;
for he went forth,
the Lord of angels,
in the strong city,
and bade fetch
angels all bright
and even bade say
to Simon Peter
that he might on Galilee
behold God
eternal and firm,
as he ere did.
Then as I understand, went
the disciples together
all to Galilee,
inspired by the Spirit,
The holy Son of God,
whom they saw
were the Lord's son.
Then over against the disciples stood
the Lord Eternal,
God in Galilee,
so that the disciples
thither all ran
Where the eternal was,
fell on the earth,
and at his feet bowed,
thanking the Lord
that thus it befell

that they should behold
the creator of angels.
Then forthwith spake
Simon Peter and said,
Art thou thus, Lord,
with power gifted?
We saw thee
at one time when
they laid thee
in loathsome bondage,
the heathen with their hands.
That they may rue
when they their end
shall behold hereafter.

. . . . .

He on the tree ascended
and shed his blood,
God on the cross
through his Spirit's power.
Wherefore we should
at all times
give to the Lord thanks
in deeds and works
for that he us from thraldom
led home
up to Heaven,
where we may share
the greatness of God."[1]

[1] Thorpe's " Cædmon's Paraphrase."—*Society of Antiquaries, London,* 1832.

[*Facing page* 49.

§ 2. About the time of Cædmon's death, early in the eighth century, the learned Eadhelm, bishop of Sherborne, was working in Glastonbury Abbey translating the Psalms of David into Anglo-Saxon, and at his request, it is said, Egbert, bishop of Holy Island, completed about the same time a version of the Gospels, of which a copy is still preserved in the British Museum.

§ 3. But the names of Eadhelm and Egbert are overshadowed by that of a contemporary far greater than either.

It was a calm peaceful evening in the spring of 735—the evening of Ascension Day—and in his quiet cell in the monastery of Jarrow an aged monk lay dying. With laboured utterance he tried to dictate to his scribe, while a group of fair-haired Saxon youths stood sorrowfully by, with tears beseeching their "dear master" to rest.

That dying monk was the most famous scholar of his day in Western Europe. Through him Jarrow-on-the-Tyne had become the great centre of literature and science, hundreds of eager students crowding yearly to its halls to learn of the famous Bæda. He was deeply versed in the literature of Greece and Rome—he had written on medicine, and astronomy, and rhetoric, and most of the other known sciences of the time—his "Ecclesiastical History" is still the chief source of our knowledge of ancient England;— but none of his studies were to him equal to the

D

study of religion, none of his books of the same
importance as his commentaries and sermons on
Scripture. Even then as he lay on his deathbed he
was feebly dictating to his scribe a translation of
St. John's Gospel. "I don't want my boys to read a
lie," he said, "or to work to no purpose after I am
gone."

And those "boys" seem to have dearly loved the
gentle old man. An epistle has come down to us
from his disciple Cuthbert to a "fellow-reader" Cuth-
win, telling of what had happened this Ascension Day.
"Our father and master, whom God loved," he says,
"had translated the Gospel of St. John as far as
'what are these among so many,' when the day came
before Our Lord's Ascension.

"He began then to suffer much in his breath, and
a swelling came in his feet, but he went on dictating
to his scribe. 'Go on quickly,' he said, 'I know not
how long I shall hold out, or how soon my Master will
call me hence.'

"All night long he lay awake in thanksgiving, and when the Ascension Day dawned, he commanded us to write with all speed what he had
begun."

Thus the letter goes on affectionately, describing
the working and resting right through the day till
the evening came, and then, with the setting sun
gilding the windows of his cell, the old man lay feebly
dictating the closing words.

"There remains but one chapter, master," said

the anxious scribe, "but it seems very hard for you to speak."

"Nay, it is easy," Bede replied; "take up thy pen and write quickly."

Amid blinding tears the young scribe wrote on. "And now, father," said he, as he eagerly caught the last words from his quivering lips, "only one sentence remains." Bede dictated it.

"It is finished, master!" cried the youth, raising his head as the last word was written.

"Ay, it is finished!" echoed the dying saint; "lift me up, place me at that window of my cell where I have so often prayed to God. Now glory be to the Father, and to the Son, and to the Holy Ghost!" and with these words the beautiful spirit passed to the presence of the Eternal Trinity.

§ 4. Our next translator is no less a person than King Alfred the Great, whose patriotic wish has been so often quoted, "that all the freeborn youth of his kingdom should employ themselves on nothing till they could first read well the English Scripture." [1]

A striking monument of his zeal for the Bible remains in the beginning of his Laws of England. The document is headed "Alfred's Dooms," and begins thus: "The dooms which the Almighty Himself spake to Moses, and gave him to keep, and after our Saviour

---

[1] At least so it is quoted, though the last words "Englisc ge-writ arædan" quite as probably mean "to read English *writing*." See Eadie's Bibl. Hist., i. 13.

Christ came to earth, He said He came not to break or forbid, but to keep them." And then follow the Ten Commandments, in the forcible simple Anglo-Saxon terms, the first part of the ancient laws of England :—

Drihten wæs sprecende thæs word to Moyse and thus cwæth :

Ic eam Drihten thy God. Ic the sit gelædde of Aegypta londe and of heora theowdome.

Ne lufa thu othre fremde godas ofer me.

* * * * *

Ara thinum fæder and thinre meder tha the Drihten sealde the, that thu sy thy leng libbende on eorthan.

Ne slea thu.

Ne stala thu.

Ne lige thu dearnunga.

Ne sæge thu lease gewitnesse with thinum nehstan.

Ne wilna thu thines nehstan yifes mid unrihte.

Ne wyrc thu the gyldene godas ohthe seolfrene.

Lord was speaking these words to Moses and thus said :

I am the Lord thy God. I led thee out of the land of Egypt and its thraldom.

Love thou not other strange gods over me.

* * * * *

Honour thy father and thy mother whom the Lord gave thee, that thou be long living on earth.

Slay not thou.

Steal not thou.

Commit not thou adultery.

Say not thou false witness against thy neighbour.

Desire not thou thy neighbour's inheritance with unright.

Work not thou thee golden gods or silvern.

Here is the Lord's Prayer of King Alfred's time :—

Uren Fader dhic art in heofnas,
  Our Father which art in heaven,

Sic gehalged dhin noma,
  Hallowed be thy name.

To cymedh dhin ric,
  Come thy kingdom,

Sic dhin uuilla sue is in heofnas and in eardho,
Be thy will so as in heaven and in earth,

Vren hlaf ofer uuirthe sel vs to daeg,
Our loaf supersubstantial give us to-day,

And forgef us scylda urna,
And forgive us   our debts,

Sue uue forgefan sculdgun vrum,
So   as we forgive   our debts,

And no inleadh vridk in costnung al gefrig
And not inlead   us into temptation but deliver

vrich   from ifle.
every one from evil.

It is interesting, as showing the growth of the
English language, to compare this with the Lord's
Prayer of 300 years afterwards :—

Fader oure that art in heve,
I-halgeed be thi nome,
I-cume thi kinereiche,
Y-worthe thi wylle also is in hevene so be on erthe,
Our iche-days-bred gif us to-day,
And forgif us oure gultes,
Also we forgifet oure gultare,

And ne led ows nowth into fondyngge,

Auth ales ows of harme,

So be hit.

Alfred also engaged in a translation of the Psalms,
which, with the Gospels, seemed the favourite Scriptures
of the people; but, unlike his great predecessor, Bede,
he died before his task was finished.

§ 5. Archbishop Ælfric, and a few other translators,
appear about the close of the tenth century, but there
is no need of describing their works in detail.   As far
as we can judge from the existing manuscripts, most
of these early Bible translations were intended for
reading in the churches to the people, and their simple
expressive terms made them very easily understood.
For example, a centurion was a "hundred-man," a
disciple a "leorning cnight," or "learning youth;"
"the man with the dropsy," is translated as "the
water-seoc-man," the Sabbath as "the reste daeg"
(rest day), and the woman who put her mites in the
treasury, is said to have cast them into the "gold-
hoard."[1]

The following specimen interestingly exhibits the
connection of this old Saxon with our modern English,
the translation being worded with a view to preserving
the similarity.

[1] See Forshall and Madden's Anglo-Saxon Gospels.

St. Matt. vii. 26, 27.

And aelc thaera the gehyrath thas mine word
And each of them that ge-heareth these mine words

and tha ne wyrcth   se bith gelic tham
and that not worketh (them) he beeth ge-like that

dysigan   man tha getimbrode **hys** hus ofer
foolish (dizzy) man that timbered his house over

sand-ceosel. Tha rinde hyt and thaer comun flod
sand-gravel. Then rained it and there come flood

and bleowun windas and ahruron on that hus, and
and blew winds and rushed on that house, and

that hus feoll and hys hryre wæs mycel.
that house fell and his fall was mickle.

CHAPTER V.

WYCLIFFE'S VERSION.

§ 1. Growth of the Language. § 2. The Parish Priest of Lutterworth. § 3. His Death. § 4. The Wycliffe Version. § 5.
Results of his Work.

§ 1 AFTER the early Anglo-Saxon versions comes a
long pause in the history of Bible translation. Amid
the disturbance resulting from the Danish invasion
there was little time for thinking of translations and
manuscripts; and before the land had fully regained
its quiet the fatal battle of Hastings had been fought,
and England lay helpless at the Normans' feet. The
higher Saxon clergy were replaced by the priests of
Normandy, who had little sympathy with the people
over whom they came, and the Saxon manuscripts
were contemptuously flung aside as relics of a rude
barbarism. The contempt shown to the language of
the defeated race quite destroyed the impulse to English
translation, and the Norman clergy had no sympathy
with the desire for spreading the knowledge of the
Scriptures among the people, so that for centuries
those Scriptures remained in England a "spring shut
up, a fountain sealed."

Yet this time must not be considered altogether lost, for during those centuries England was becoming fitted for an English Bible. The future language of the nation was being formed ; the Saxon and Norman French were struggling side by side ; gradually the old Saxon grew unintelligible to the people ; gradually the French became a foreign tongue, and with the fusion of the two races a language grew up which was the language of united England.[1]

§ 2. Passing, then, from the quiet deathbeds of Alfred and Bede, we transfer ourselves to the great hall of the Blackfriars' Monastery, London, on a dull, warm May day in 1378, amid purple robes and gowns of satin and

---

[1] "In tracing the history of the change from Anglo-Saxon to modern English it is impossible to assign any precise dates by which we can mark the origin of this change, or the principal epochs of its progress, or its completion. This necessarily results from the very gradual nature of the change itself ; we might as well ask at what moment a child becomes a youth, or a youth a man ; or when the plant becomes a tree. So gradual was the change, that, to adopt the language of Hallam, 'When we compare the earliest English of the thirteenth century with the Anglo-Saxon of the twelfth, it seems hard to pronounce why it should pass for a separate language rather than a modification and simplification of the former.' Still, for the sake of convenience, we may fix on certain dates somewhere about which the change commenced or was effected. About 1150, or a little less than a century after the Conquest, may be dated the decline of pure Saxon ; about 1250, or a century later, the commencement of English. During the intervening century the language has been called by many of our writers semi-Saxon."—*H. Rogers in Edinburgh Review, Oct.* 1850.

It was towards the end of the fourteenth century that English began to be the language of literature. "Sir John Mandeville's Travels," one of the earliest English books, appeared in 1356, and Chaucer wrote towards the close of the century ; therefore Wycliffe's Bible in 1383 was about as early as a version could be which was to retain its place among the English people.

damask, amid monks and abbots, and bishops and
doctors of the Church, assembled for the trial of John
Wycliffe, the parish priest of Lutterworth.

The great hall, crowded to its heavy oaken doors,
witnesses to the interest that is centred in the trial,
and all eyes are fixed on the pale stern old man who
stands before the dais silently facing his judges.   He
is quite alone, and his thoughts go back, with some
bitterness, to his previous trial, when the people crowded
the doors shouting for their favourite, and John of
Gaunt and the Lord Marshal of England were standing
by his side.   He has learned since then not to put his
trust in princes.   The power of his enemies has rapidly
grown, even the young King has been won over to their
cause, and patrons and friends have drawn back from
his side, whom the Church has resolved to crush.

The judges have taken their seats, and the accused
stands awaiting the charges to be read, when suddenly
there is a quick cry of terror.   A strange rumbling
sound fills the air, and the walls of the judgment-hall
are trembling to their base—the monastery and the city
of London are being shaken by an earthquake!   Friar
and prelate grow pale with superstitious awe.   Twice
already has the arraignment of Wycliffe been strangely
interrupted.   Are the elements in league with this
enemy of the Church?   Shall they give up the trial?

"No!" thunders Archbishop Courtenay, rising in his
place, "we will not give up the trial.   This earthquake
but portends the purging of the kingdom; for as there
are in the bowels of the earth noxious vapours which

only by a violent earthquake can be purged away, so are there evils brought by such men upon this land which only by a very earthquake can ever be removed. Let the trial go forward ! "

What think you, reader, were the evils which this pale ascetic had wrought, needing a very earthquake to cleanse them from the land? Had he falsified the Divine Message to the people in his charge? Was he turning men's hearts from the worship of God? Was his priestly office disgraced by carelessness or drunkenness or impurity of life?

Oh no. Such faults could be gently judged at the tribunal in the Blackfriars' Hall. Wycliffe's was a far more serious crime. He had dared to attack the corruptions of the Church, and especially the enormities of the begging friars—he had indignantly denounced Pardons and Indulgences and Masses for the soul as part of a system of gigantic fraud ; and worst of all, he had filled up the cup of his iniquity by translating the Scriptures into the English tongue, " making it," as one of the chroniclers[1] angrily complains, " common and more open to laymen and to women than it was wont to be to clerks well learned and of good understanding, so that the pearl of the Gospel is trodden under foot of swine."

The feeling of his opponents will be better understood if we notice the position of the Church in England at the time. The meridian of her power had been already passed. Her clergy as a class were

[1] Kneighton.

ignorant and corrupt. Her people were neglected, except for the money to be extorted by Masses and Pardons, "as if," to quote the words of an old writer, "God had given His sheep not be pastured but to be shaven and shorn." This state of things had gone on for centuries, and the people like dumb driven cattle had submitted. But those who could discern the signs of the times must have seen now that it could not go on much longer. The spread of education was rapidly increasing, several new colleges having been founded in Oxford during Wycliffe's lifetime. A strong spirit of independence, too, was rising among the people— already Edward III. and his Parliament had indignantly refused the Pope's demand for the annual tribute to be sent to Rome. It was evident that a crisis was near. And, as if to hasten the crisis, the famous schism of the Papacy had placed two Popes at the head of the Church, and all Christendom was scandalised by the sight of the rival "vicars of Jesus Christ" anathematising each other from Rome and Avignon, raising armies and slaughtering helpless women and children, each for the aggrandising of himself.

The minds of men in England were greatly agitated, and Wycliffe felt that at such a time the firmest charter of the Church would be the open Bible in her children's hands; the best exposure of the selfish policy of her rulers, the exhibiting to the people the beautiful self-forgetting life of Jesus Christ as recorded in the Gospels. "The Sacred Scriptures," he said, "are the property of the people, and one which no one should be allowed to wrest from them. . . . Christ and His apostles converted the world by making known the Scriptures to men in a form familiar to them, . . . and I pray with all my heart that through doing the things contained in this book we may all together come to the everlasting life.'\ This Bible translation he placed far the first in importance of all his attempts to reform the English Church, and he pursued his object with a vigour and against an opposition that reminds one of the old monk of Bethlehem and his Bible a thousand years before.

The result of the Blackfriars' Synod was, that after three days' deliberation Wycliffe's teaching was condemned, and at a subsequent meeting he himself was excommunicated. He returned to his quiet parsonage at Lutterworth—for his enemies dared not yet proceed to extremities—and there, with his pile of old Latin manuscripts and commentaries, he laboured on at the great work of his life, till the whole Bible was translated into the " modir tonge," and England received for the first time in her history a complete version of the Scriptures [1] in the language of the people.

---

[1] This honour has by some been denied to Wycliffe, chiefly on the authority of Sir Thomas More. "Ye schall understande," he says, "that yᵉ great arch heretike John Wycliffe, whereas yᵉ Holy Bible was long before his dayes by vertuous and well lerned men translated into yᵉ Englische tong and by good and godly people with devotion and soberness well and reverently read, tooke upon him of malicious purpose to translate it anew. In whiche translacioun he purposely corrupted yᵉ Holy Text, maliciously planting therein such wordes as might in yᵉ reders' eres serve to the profe of such heresies as he was aboute to sowe. . . Myself haue seen and can shew you Bibles fayre

§ 3. And scarce was his task well finished when, like his great predecessor Bede, the brave old priest laid down his life. He himself had expected that a violent death would have finished his course. His enemies were many and powerful; the primate, the king, and the Pope were against him, with the friars, whom he had so often and so fiercely defied;[1] so that his destruction seemed but a mere question of time. But while his enemies were preparing to strike, the old man "was not, for God took him."

It was the close of the Old Year, the last Sunday of 1384, and his little flock at Lutterworth were kneeling in hushed reverence before the altar, when suddenly, at the time of the elevation of the Sacrament, he fell to the ground in a violent fit of the palsy, and never spoke again until his death on the last day of the year.

In him England lost one of her best and greatest

and olde, written in Englische, which have been known and seen by ye bischop of ye dyoces and left in lemen's hands and women's."

However, he gives us no means of testing his statement, and the fullest investigation gives no trace of anything but separate fragments of Scripture before Wycliffe's time. Perhaps Sir Thomas More had seen some of Wycliffe's own copies, and mistook them for the work of another and earlier writer, or more probably the statement was made hastily and without proper foundation. A few partial translations had been accomplished in the century before Wycliffe by Scorham, Rolle of Hampole, and others, but they were little known. Wycliffe's great complaint is that there is no English translation of the Scriptures.

[1] The scene has frequently been described of the friars pressing round what seemed the death-bed of their old assailant, adjuring him to recant and receive their absolution, and the stern old man raising himself suddenly to startle them with his fierce prophetic cry, "I shall not die, but live to declare again the evil deeds of the friars!"

sons, a patriot sternly resenting all dishonour to his country, a reformer who ventured his life for the purity of the Church and the freedom of the Bible —an earnest, faithful " parsoun of a toune " standing out conspicuously among the clergy of the time,

> " For Cristè's lore and his apostles twelve
> He taughte—and first he folwede it himselve." [1]

Here is a choice specimen from one of the monkish writers of the time describing his death :—" On the feast of the passion of St. Thomas of Canterbury, John Wycliffe, the organ of the devil, the enemy of the Church, the idol of heretics, the image of hypocrites, the restorer of schism, the storehouse of lies, the sink of flattery, being struck by the horrible judgment of God, was seized with the palsy throughout his whole body, and that mouth which was to have spoken huge things against God and His saints, and holy Church, was miserably drawn aside, and afforded a frightful spectacle to beholders ; his tongue was speechless and his head shook, showing plainly that the curse which God had thundered forth against Cain was also inflicted on him." [2]

Some time after his death a petition was presented to the Pope, which to his honour he rejected, praying him to order Wycliffe's body to be taken out of conse- crated ground and buried in a dunghill. But forty years after, by a decree of the Council of Constance, the

---

[1] Chaucer's *Prologue*, 527. The whole of that exquisite description of the "parsoun" is supposed to refer to Wycliffe, whose teaching the poet had warmly embraced.   [2] Lewis's " Life of Wycliffe."

old Reformer's bones were dug up and burnt, and the ashes flung into the little river Swift, which "runneth hard by his church at Lutterworth." And so, in the often-quoted words of old Fuller, "as the Swift bare them into the Severn, and the Severn into the narrow seas, and they again into the ocean, thus the ashes of Wycliffe is an emblem of his doctrine, which is now dispersed over all the world."

§ 4. But it is with his Bible translation that we are specially concerned. As far as we can learn, the whole Bible was not translated by the Reformer. About half the Old Testament is ascribed to Nicholas de Hereford,[1] one of the Oxford leaders of the Lollards, the remainder, with the whole of the New Testament, being done by Wycliffe himself. About eight years after its completion the whole was revised by Richard Purvey, his curate and intimate friend, whose manuscript is still in the library of Trinity College, Dublin. Purvey's preface is a most interesting old document, and shows not only

---

[1] He appears to have stopped abruptly in the middle of the verse (Baruch iii. 20), probably at the time of his seizure for heresy. Here is a specimen of his translation, Psalm xxiii. :—"The Lord gouerneth me and no thing to me shal lacke ; in the place of leswe where he me ful sette. Ouer watir of fulfilling he nurshide me ; my soule he conuertide. He broghte down upon me the sties of rightwiseness ; for his name. For whi and if I shal go in the myddel of the shadewe of deth ; I shal not dreden euelis, for thou art with me. Thi yerde and thi staf ; the han confortid me. Thou hast maad redi in thi sighte a bord ; aghen them that trublyn me. Thou hast myche fatted in oile myn hed and my chalis makende ful drunken, hou right cler it is. And thi mercy shall vnderfolewe me ; alle the dayis of my lif. And that I dwelle in the hous of the Lord in to the lengthe of dayis."

that he was deeply in earnest about his work, but that he thoroughly understood the intellectual and moral conditions necessary for its success.

"A simpel creature," he says, "hath translated the Scripture out of Latin into Englische. First, this simpel creature had much travayle with divers fellows and helpers to gather many old Bibles and other doctors and glosses to make one Latin Bible some deal true and then to study it anew the texte and any other help he might get, especially Lyra on the Old Testament, which helped him much with this work. The third time to counsel with olde grammarians and old divines of hard words and hard sentences how they might best be understood and translated, the fourth time to translate as clearly as he could to the sense, and to have many good fellows and cunnyng at the correcting of the translacioun. . . . A translator hath great nede to studie well the sense both before and after, and then also he hath nede to live a clene life and be full devout in preiers, and have not his wit occupied about worldli things that the Holy Spyrit author of all wisdom and cunnynge and truthe dresse him for his work and suffer him not to err." And he concludes with the prayer, "God grant to us all grace to ken well and to kepe well Holie Writ, and to suffer joiefulli some paine for it at the laste."

Like all the earlier English translations, Wycliffe's Bible was based on the Latin Vulgate of St. Jerome; and this is the great defect in his work, as compared with the versions that followed. He was not capable of

E

consulting the original Greek and Hebrew even if he had access to them—in fact, there was probably no man in England at the time capable of doing so; and therefore, though he represents the Latin faithfully and well, he of course handed on its errors as faithfully as its perfections. But, such as it is, it is a fine specimen of fourteenth century English. He translated not for scholars or for nobles, but for the plain people, and his style was such as suited those for whom he wrote—plain, vigorous, homely, and yet with all its homeliness full of a solemn grace and dignity, which made men feel that they were reading no ordinary book. He uses many striking expressions, such as 2 Tim. ii. 4, "No man holding knighthood to God, wlappith himself with worldli nedes;" and many of the best-known phrases in our present Bible originated with him, *e.g.*, "the beame and the mote," "the depe thingis of God," "strait is the gate and narewe is the waye," "no but a man schall be born againe," "the cuppe of blessing which we blessen," &c. &c.

Here is a specimen from Wycliffe's Gospels, and it will be an interesting illustration of the growth of our language to compare it, on the one hand, with the specimens 400 years earlier given in the previous chapter, and on the other with the present Revised Version, which is later in date by 500 years. The resemblance to the latter will be still more marked if the sound only is followed, disregarding the spelling. It is somewhere recorded that at a meeting in Yorkshire recently a long passage of Wycliffe's Bible was

read, which was quite intelligible throughout to those
who heard.

MATT. III. 1-6.—𝕵𝖓 𝖙𝖍𝖎𝖑𝖐𝖊 𝖉𝖆𝖞𝖊𝖘 𝖈𝖆𝖒𝖊 𝕵𝖔𝖔𝖓
𝕭𝖆𝖕𝖙𝖎𝖘𝖙 𝖕𝖗𝖊𝖈𝖍𝖞𝖓𝖌𝖊 𝖎𝖓 𝖙𝖍𝖊 𝖉𝖊𝖘𝖊𝖗𝖙 𝖔𝖋 𝕵𝖚𝖉𝖊,
𝖘𝖆𝖞𝖎𝖓𝖌, 𝕯𝖔 𝖞𝖊 𝖕𝖊𝖓𝖆𝖚𝖓𝖈𝖊: 𝖋𝖔𝖗 𝖙𝖍𝖊 𝖐𝖞𝖓𝖌𝖉𝖔𝖒
𝖔𝖋 𝖍𝖊𝖚𝖊𝖓𝖘 𝖘𝖍𝖆𝖑𝖑 𝖓𝖊𝖎𝖌𝖍. 𝕱𝖔𝖗𝖘𝖔𝖙𝖍𝖊 𝖙𝖍𝖎𝖘 𝖎𝖘
𝖍𝖊 𝖔𝖋 𝖜𝖍𝖔𝖒 𝖎𝖙 𝖎𝖘 𝖘𝖆𝖎𝖉 𝖇𝖞 𝕻𝖘𝖆𝖞𝖊 𝖙𝖍𝖊 𝖕𝖗𝖔=
𝖕𝖍𝖊𝖙𝖊, 𝕬 𝖛𝖔𝖎𝖈𝖊 𝖔𝖋 𝖆 𝖈𝖗𝖞𝖎𝖓𝖌𝖊 𝖎𝖓 𝖉𝖊𝖘𝖊𝖗𝖙, 𝕸𝖆𝖐𝖊
𝖞𝖊 𝖗𝖊𝖉𝖞 𝖙𝖍𝖊 𝖜𝖆𝖞𝖊𝖘 𝖔𝖋 𝖙𝖍𝖊 𝕷𝖔𝖗𝖉, 𝖒𝖆𝖐𝖊 𝖞𝖊
𝖗𝖎𝖌𝖍𝖙𝖋𝖚𝖑 𝖙𝖍𝖊 𝖕𝖆𝖙𝖍𝖊𝖘 𝖔𝖋 𝖍𝖞𝖒. 𝕱𝖔𝖗𝖘𝖔𝖙𝖍𝖊 𝖙𝖍𝖆𝖙
𝖎𝖑𝖐𝖊 𝕵𝖔𝖔𝖓 𝖍𝖆𝖉𝖉𝖊 𝖈𝖑𝖔𝖙𝖍 𝖔𝖋 𝖙𝖍𝖊 𝖍𝖊𝖊𝖗𝖎𝖘 𝖔𝖋
𝖈𝖆𝖒𝖊𝖞𝖑𝖎𝖘 𝖆𝖓𝖉 𝖆 𝖌𝖎𝖗𝖉𝖎𝖑 𝖔𝖋 𝖘𝖐𝖞𝖓 𝖆𝖇𝖔𝖚𝖙 𝖍𝖎𝖘
𝖑𝖊𝖊𝖓𝖉𝖎𝖘; 𝖘𝖔𝖙𝖍𝖊𝖑𝖞 𝖍𝖎𝖘 𝖒𝖊𝖙𝖊 𝖜𝖊𝖗𝖊𝖓 𝖑𝖔𝖈𝖚𝖘𝖙𝖎𝖘
𝖆𝖓𝖉 𝖍𝖔𝖓𝖞 𝖔𝖋 𝖙𝖍𝖊 𝖜𝖔𝖉𝖊. 𝕮𝖍𝖆𝖓𝖓𝖊 𝕵𝖊𝖗𝖚𝖘𝖆=
𝖑𝖊𝖒 𝖜𝖊𝖓𝖙𝖊 𝖔𝖚𝖙 𝖙𝖔 𝖍𝖞𝖒, 𝖆𝖓𝖉 𝖆𝖑 𝕵𝖚𝖉𝖊, 𝖆𝖓𝖉 𝖆𝖑
𝖙𝖍𝖊 𝖈𝖚𝖓𝖙𝖗𝖊 𝖆𝖇𝖔𝖚𝖙𝖊 𝕵𝖔𝖗𝖉𝖆𝖓, 𝖆𝖓𝖉 𝖙𝖍𝖊𝖎 𝖜𝖊𝖗𝖊𝖓
𝖈𝖗𝖞𝖘𝖙𝖊𝖓𝖊𝖉 𝖔𝖋 𝖍𝖞𝖒 𝖎𝖓 𝕵𝖔𝖗𝖉𝖆𝖓, 𝖐𝖓𝖔𝖜𝖑𝖊𝖈𝖍𝖞𝖓𝖌𝖊
𝖙𝖍𝖊𝖗𝖊 𝖘𝖞𝖓𝖓𝖊𝖘.

It will be seen that this specimen is not divided
into verses. Verse division belongs to a much later
period,[1] and though convenient for reference, it sometimes a good deal spoils the sense. The division into

---

[1] It first appears in the Geneva Bible, 1560. See pp. 102-3. We
owe it to Robert Stephen, the celebrated editor of the Greek Testament, who hurriedly arranged it on a journey from Paris to Lyons.
"I think," a commentator quaintly remarks, "it had been better done
on his knees in the closet."

chapters appears in Wycliffe's as in our own Bibles. This chapter division had shortly before been made by a Cardinal Hugo, for the purpose of a Latin Concordance, and its convenience brought it quickly into use. But, like the verse division, it is often very badly done, the object aimed at seeming to be uniformity of length rather than any natural division of the subject.[1] Sometimes a chapter breaks off in the middle of a narrative or an argument, and, especially in St. Paul's epistles, the incorrect division often becomes misleading. The removal as far as possible of these divisions is one of the advantages of the Revised Version to be noticed later on.

§ 5. The book had a very wide circulation. While the Anglo-Saxon versions were confined for the most part to the few religious houses where they were written, Wycliffe's Bible, in spite of its disadvantage of being only manuscript, was circulated largely through the kingdom; and though the cost a good deal restricted its possession to the wealthier classes,[2] those who could

[1] Compare, for example, the beginnings of Matt. x., xx. ; Mark iii., ix. ; Luke xxi. ; Acts viii. ; 1 Cor. xi. ; 2 Cor. v., vii., &c. &c.   An awkward division for a clergyman reading the lessons is at end of Acts xxi., where, however he may manage his voice, it is difficult to avoid reading, "Paul spake in the Hebrew tongue, saying, Here endeth the second lesson." The Irish Church Lectionary has altered this lesson.

[2] Even now, after 500 years, one hundred and seventy of these copies remain, some of them of great interest from the inscriptions on their title-pages. One bears the name of Henry VI., another of Richard, the crookbacked Duke of Gloucester, others belonged to Henry VII. and Edward VI., and one has an inscription telling that it was presented to Queen Elizabeth as a birthday gift by one of her chaplains.

not hope to possess it gained access to it too, as well through their own efforts as through the ministrations of Wycliffe's "pore priestes." A considerable sum was paid for even a few sheets of the manuscript, a load of hay was given for permission to read it for a certain period one hour a day,[1] and those who could not afford even such expenses adopted what means they could. It is touching to read such incidents as that of one Alice Collins, sent for to the little gatherings "to recite the ten commandments and parts of the Epistles of SS. Paul and Peter, which she knew by heart." "Certes," says old John Foxe in his "Book of Martyrs," "the zeal of those Christian days seems much superior to this of our day, and to see the travail of them may well shame our careless times."

But it was at a terrible risk such study was carried on. The appearance of Wycliffe's Bible aroused at once

[1] The readers, as might be expected, often surreptitiously copying portions of special interest. One is reminded of the story in ancient Irish history of a curious decision arising out of an incident of this kind nearly a thousand years before, which seems to have influenced the history of Christianity in Britain. St. Columb, on a visit to the aged St. Finian in Ulster, had permission to read in the Psalter belonging to his host. But every night while the good old saint was sleeping, the young one was busy in the chapel writing by a miraculous light till he had completed a copy of the whole Psalter. The owner of the Psalter discovering this, demanded that it should be given up, as it had been copied unlawfully from his book; while the copyist insisted that, the materials and labour being his, he was entitled to what he had written. The dispute was referred to Diarmad the king at Tara, and his decision (genuinely Irish) was given in St. Finian's favour. "To every book," said he, "belongs its son-book (copy), *as to every cow belongs her calf.*" Columb complained of the decision as unjust, and the dispute is said to have been one of the causes of his leaving Ireland for Iona (see note, p 43).

fierce opposition. A bill was brought into Parliament
to forbid the circulation of the Scriptures in English;
but the sturdy John of Gaunt vigorously asserted the
right of the people to have the Word of God in their
own tongue; "for why," said he, "are we to be the
dross of the nations?" However, the rulers of the
Church grew more and more alarmed at the circulation
of the book. At length Archbishop Arundel, a zealous
but not very learned prelate, complained to the Pope of
"that pestilent wretch, John Wycliffe, the son of the
old Serpent, the forerunner of Antichrist, who had completed his iniquity by inventing a new translation of
the Scriptures;" and shortly after the Convocation of
Canterbury forbade such translations, under penalty of
the major excommunication.[1]

"God grant us," runs the prayer in the old Bible preface, "to ken and to kepe well Holie Writ, and to suffer
joiefulli some paine for it at the laste." What a meaning that prayer must have gained when the readers of
the book were burned with the copies round their necks,
when men and women were executed for teaching their
children the Lord's Prayer and ten commandments in

[1] Their reasons were worthy of the enlightened Archbishop who was
at their head. "It is a dangerous thing, as witnesseth blessed St.
Jerome, to translate the text of the Scripture out of one tongue into
another, for in the translation the sense is not always easily kept. We
therefore decree and ordain that no man hereafter by his own authority
translate any text of the Scripture into English or any other tongue by
way of book, pamphlet, or treatise, and that no man read any such
book, pamphlet, or treatise now lately composed in the time of John
Wycliffe, or hereafter to be set forth, under pain of the major excommunication, until the said translation be approved by the ordinary of
the place or the Council Provincial."

English, when husbands were made to witness against
their wives, and children forced to light the death-fires
of their parents, and possessors of the banned Wycliffe
Bible were hunted down as if they were wild beasts.

Thus did Wycliffe, in his effort for the spread of the
Gospel of Peace, bring, like his Master fourteen centuries
before, "not peace but a sword." Every bold attempt
to let in the light on long-standing darkness seems to
result first in a fierce opposition from the evil creatures
that delight in the darkness, and the weak creatures
weakened by dwelling in it so long. It is not till the
driving back of the evil and the strengthening of the
weak, as the light gradually wins its way, that the true
results can be seen. It is, to use a simile of a graceful
modern writer,[1] as when you raise with your staff an old
flat stone, with the grass forming a little hedge, as it
were, around it as it lies. "Beneath it, what a revelation! Blades of grass flattened down, colourless,
matted together, as if they had been bleached and
ironed; hideous crawling things; black crickets with
their long filaments sticking out on all sides; motion-
less, slug-like creatures; young larvæ, perhaps more
horrible in their pulpy stillness than in the infernal
wriggle of maturity. But no sooner is the stone turned
and the wholesome light of day let in on this com-
pressed and blinded community of creeping things than
all of them that have legs rush blindly about, butting
against each other and everything else in their way,

---

[1] Oliver Wendell Holmes, in the "Autocrat of the Breakfast-table."

and end in a general stampede to underground retreats from the region poisoned by sunshine. Next year you will find the grass growing fresh and green where the stone lay—the ground bird builds her nest where the beetle had his hole, the dandelion and the buttercup are growing there, and the broad fans of insect-angels open and shut over their golden discs as the rhythmic waves of blissful consciousness pulsate through their glorified being.

"The stone is ancient error, the grass is human nature borne down and bleached of all its colour by it, the shapes that are found beneath are the crafty beings that thrive in the darkness and the weak organisations kept helpless by it. He who turns the stone is whosoever puts the staff of truth to the old lying incubus, whether he do it with a serious face or a laughing one. The next year stands for the coming time. Then shall the nature which had lain blanched and broken rise in its full stature and native lines in the sunshine. Then shall God's minstrels build their nests in the hearts of a new-born humanity. Then shall beauty—divinity taking outline and colour—light upon the souls of men as the butterfly, image of the beatified spirit rising from the dust, soars from the shell that held a poor grub, which would never have found wings unless that stone had been lifted."

CHAPTER VI.

TYNDALE'S VERSION.

§ 1. Printing. § 2. Revival of Greek Learning. § 3. Tyndale's Work. § 4. Reception of the Book in England. § 5. Death of Tyndale. § 6. Description of Tyndale's Version.

§ 1. AFTER Wycliffe there is an interval of a hundred years before we come to the next great version of the Bible, but in that interval occurred what more than any other event that ever happened has affected the history of the English Bible, and indeed the history of the English nation altogether. Up to this time in wild Iona, in the monasteries of ancient Britain, in the great homes of learning through the continent of Europe, men and women sat in the silence of their cells slowly copying out letter by letter the pages of the Scripture manuscripts, watching patiently month after month the volumes grow beneath their hands. But with Wycliffe's days this toilsome manuscript period closes for ever.

About twenty years after the death of Wycliffe there was living in the old German town of Mentz a boy bearing the not very attractive name of Johann Gensfleisch, which means, put into plain English, John Gooseflesh. One morning—so runs the story—he had

been cutting the letters of his name out of the bark
of a tree, and having been left alone in the house soon
after, amused himself by spreading out the letters on
a board so as to form again the words,

Johann Gensfleisch.

A pot of purple dye was beside the fire, and by some
awkward turn one of his letters dropped into it. Quickly,
without stopping to think, he snatched it out of the
boiling liquid, and as quickly let it drop again, this time
on a white dressed skin which lay on a bench near by,
the result being a beautiful purple h on a deep yellowish
white ground. Whether the boy admired the beautiful marks on the skin or meditated ruefully of future
marks on his own skin as a possible consequence history does not record, but it would seem as if somehow
that image rooted itself in his mind, to bear rich fruit on
a future day. For, thirty years afterward, when all
Germany was ringing with the name of Johann Gutenberg and his magical art of printing, the good people
of Mentz recognised in the inventor their young
townsman Gensfleisch, who had meantime taken his
maternal name.[1] Whatever truth there may be in the
legend, certain it is that Gutenberg's printing press
was working in Mentz about the year 1450, and the
first completed book that issued from that press is said
to have been the Latin Bible.[2]

---

[1] He was the son of Frilo Gensfleisch and Elsie Gutenberg. The
German law recognised in certain cases this taking of the maternal
name.

[2] It is known as the Mazarin Bible, from the fact that a copy of it
was found about a century ago in Cardinal Mazarin's library at Paris.

This is not the place to tell what has been so often told already of the immense influence of this new invention on the progress of knowledge in the world. We have but to do with its effects as manifested in the history of the Bible, and for this it will be sufficient to remark that the Bible which took Wycliffe's copyists ten months to prepare can now be produced by a single London firm at the rate of 120 per hour, that is, two copies every minute; while, for cost of production, we may compare the Wycliffe Bible at a price equal to £40 of our money,[1] with a New Testament complete in paper covers that has lately been published for one penny!

§ 2. Another event of the same period of very great importance in our Bible history was the revival of Greek learning in Europe. The reader will remember that up to this time our pile of " ANCIENT MANUSCRIPTS " remains untouched, the English Scriptures being translated not from the original Greek and Hebrew, but from the Latin Vulgate, which itself, as we have seen, was only a translation.[2] For many centuries Greek was practically unknown in Western Europe, but about this time gradually the study was revived. "Greece," it has been finely said, "rose from the grave with the

---

[1] Mr. Froude ("Hist. Eng.") has some interesting pages to show the value of money in those days. A pig or a goose was bought for 4d., a chicken for 1d., a hen for 2d.; land was let at 8d. per acre; labourers were hired at 1d. per day; the stipend of a parish priest was £5, 6s. 8d. a year; and Bradford, the martyr, writes of his fellowship at Oxford, "It is worth £7 a year to me, so you see what a good lord God is to me."

[2] See Diagram facing title-page.

New Testament in her hand," and before the close of
the sixteenth century the "new learning" had become
an important part of university education in Europe.

§ 3. At this critical period came forth the man whc
was to use these new powers with such marvellous effect
in the service of the English Bible. In 1483, the year
after the birth of Luther, and a hundred years after
the death of Wycliffe, William Tyndale was born. He
grew up a thoughtful studious youth, and at an early
age won for himself in Oxford a distinguished position
for scholarship. Soon afterwards he moved to Cambridge, where he met with Erasmus, the greatest Greek
scholar of the day, who had just completed his Greek
Testament from a comparison of some ancient manuscripts. Tyndale quickly made himself familiar with
this wonderful new book. He took it up probably at
first as a curious work of scholarship, but he soon found
that there was more in it than this; and like his great
contemporary Luther, and almost at the same time, he
read again and again with ever deepening interest the
wondrous revelation of the love of God to man, till his
spirit was stirred to its depths. He could not keep his
treasure to himself. He argued with the priests, and
exhorted them to the study of the Scriptures for themselves; and it was about this time that one day, in the
sudden heat of controversy, he startled all around by
his memorable declaration, whose fulfilment was after-

ward the object of his life. "We had better," said his
opponent, "be without God's laws than the Pope's."

And Tyndale rose in his indignant wrath. "I defy the Pope," he cried, "and all his laws; and if God spare me I will one day make the boy that drives the plough in England to know more of Scripture than the Pope does." [1]

He had already translated some portions from the original Greek, and now, encouraged by the report he had heard of him as a patron of learning, he applied confidently to Cuthbert Tonstal, Bishop of London, for permission to carry on his work in the episcopal palace under his lordship's patronage. But translation of classical authors was a very different thing from translation of the Scriptures, and the bishop chillingly replied that there was no room in the palace for carrying on such a work. However, he was kindly received by Humphrey Monmouth, a London merchant, and in his house for nearly a year he assiduously, though very quietly, prosecuted his task.

But that year of contact with the ecclesiastics of the city plainly showed him that no mercy would be extended to any movement which disturbed their quiet. He saw men around him led to prison and to death for possessing or reading a copy of Luther's writings, and he knew well that a Bible translation would be a still more dangerous book. "Wherefore," he sadly says, "I perceived that not only in my lord of London's palace,

---

[1] An edition of Tyndale's Testament, prepared during his imprisonment, is sometimes spoken of as the literal fulfilment of this vow—a Testament for the ploughboys of his native county. It contains words seemingly of a provincial dialect—faether, maester, sloene, oones, whersse, &c. Most probably, however. these peculiarities are due to a Flemish proof-reader.

but in all England, there was no room for attempting a translation of the Scriptures."[1]

Tyndale was not one of those who, having put their hands to the plough, look back. He had determined that England should have the Word of God spread among her people by means of this new invention of printing, and he had calmly counted the cost. If his work could be done in England, well. If not—if only a life of exile could accomplish it—then that life of exile he would cheerfully accept. So in 1524 he left his native land, never to see it again; and at Hamburg, in poverty and distress, and amid constant danger, the brave-hearted exile worked at his translation,[2] and so diligently that the following year we find him at Cologne with the sheets of his quarto New Testament already in the printer's hands.

But a sad disappointment was in store for him. He had kept his secret well, and he hoped that in a few months more the little book would be spreading in thousands through the length and breadth of England. But just as his hopes were highest, one day there came to him a hurried message at his lodgings, and half distracted he rushed to the printer's house, seized all the sheets he could lay hands on, and fled from the town. A priest named Cochlaeus had heard an idle boast of

---

[1] Tyndale's Preface.

[2] He seems to have had no help in the translation. For correcting proofs and such work he had one Friar Roye, whom he rather humorously describes. "As long as he had no money I could somewhat rule him, but as soon as he had gotten him money he became like himself again. So as soon as I was ended I bade him farewell for our two lives, and as men say a day longer."

some printers which roused his suspicions, and by diligently plying them with wine the startling secret at
length came out that an English New Testament was
actually in the press, and already far on its way to
completion. Quite horrified at such a conspiracy,
"worse," he thought, "than that of the eunuchs against
Ahasuerus," he at once gave information to the magis-
trates, and demanded that the sheets should be seized,
while he at the same time despatched a messenger to
the English bishops to warn them of this unexpected
danger. Hence the consternation of Tyndale and his
hurried flight from Cologne.

With his precious sheets he escaped to Worms, where
the enthusiasm for Luther and the Reformation was
then at its height, and there at length he accomplished
his design, producing for the first time a complete
printed New Testament in English.[1] Knowing of the
information that Cochlaeus had given, and that in
consequence the books would be jealously watched, he
printed also an edition in smaller size, as more likely to
escape detection, and at once made provision for the

[1] Canon Westcott ("Hist. Bible") quotes an interesting account of
Tyndale's work at Worms, from the diary of a German scholar who
was a casual visitor there in 1526. After mentioning other subjects of
conversation at the dinner-table, the writer goes on to say—"One told
us that 6000 copies of the English New Testament had been printed
at Worms, that it was translated by an Englishman who lived there
with two of his countrymen, who was so complete a master of seven
languages—Hebrew, Greek, Latin, Italian, Spanish, English, French—
that you would fancy that whichever he spoke in was his native
tongue. He told us also that the English, in spite of the active opposition of the King, were so eager for the Gospel that they would buy
the New Testament even if they had to give 100,000 pieces of money
for it."

forwarding his dangerous merchandise to England. In cases, in barrels, in bales of cloth, in sacks of flour, every secret way that could be devised, the books were sent; and in spite of the utmost vigilance in watching the ports, many of them arrived and were scattered far and wide through the country.

§ 4. Such a commotion as they created among the hostile clergy! Wycliffe's Testaments had been troublesome enough, even though it took months to finish a single copy and the cost was in a great measure prohibitive. But here were books pouring into the country capable of being produced at the rate of hundreds per day, and at a price within the reach of all. Vigorous measures indeed would be necessary now!

The warning of Cochlaeus had set them on their guard, and every port was carefully watched by officers appointed for the purpose. Thousands of copies were thus seized in their various disguises, and were burned with solemn ceremony at the old cross of St. Paul's, as "a burnt-offering most pleasing to Almighty God;"[1] and still other thousands supplied their place.[2] Tyndale was but little discouraged at their efforts, for he knew that the printing press could defy them all. "In burning the book," he says, "they did none other thing than I looked for; no more shall they do if they burn me also, if it be God's will that it should be so."

It was quite clear that they could not hinder the

---

[1] Cardinal Campeggio's letter to Wolsey.

[2] About 15,000 of his first New Testament were issued within four years.

entrance of the book into England. And then a brilliant thought occurred to the Bishop of London. He sought out Augustine Pakington, a merchant trading to Antwerp, and asked his opinion about the buying up of all the copies across the water.

"My lord," replied Pakington, who was a secret friend of Tyndale, "if it be your pleasure I could do in this matter probably more than any merchant in England; so if it be your lordship's pleasure to pay for them—for I must disburse money for them—I will insure you to have every book that remains unsold."

"Gentle Master Pakington," said the bishop, 'deemyng that he hadde God by the toe, whanne in truthe he hadde, as after he thought, the devyl by the fiste,'[1] "do your diligence and get them for me, and I will gladly give you whatever they may cost, for the books are naughty, and I intend surely to destroy them all, and to burn them at Paul's Cross."

A few weeks later Pakington sought the translator, whose funds he knew were at a low ebb.

"Master Tyndale," he said, "I have found you a good purchaser for your books."

"Who is he?" asked Tyndale.

"My lord of London."

"But if the bishop wants the books it must be only to burn them."

"Well," was the reply, "what of that? The bishop will burn them anyhow, and it is best that you should have the money for the enabling you to imprint others instead."

[1] " Halle's Chronicle."

And so the bargain was made. " The bishop had the books, Pakington had the thanks, and Tyndale had the money."

" I am the gladder," quoth Tyndale, "for these two benefits shall come thereof. I shall get money to bring myself out of debt, and the whole world will cry out against the burning of God's Word, and the overplus of the money that shall remain with me shall make me more studious to correct the said New Testament, and so newly to imprint the same once again, and I trust the second will be much better than ever was the first."

The Chronicle [1] which relates the story goes on to tell that—"After this Tyndale corrected the same Testaments again, and caused them to be newly imprinted, so that they came thick and threefold into England. The bishop sent for Pakington again, and asked how the Testaments were still so abundant. 'My lord,' replied the merchant, 'it were best for your lordship to buy up the stamps too by the which they are imprinted.'"

It is with evident enjoyment that the old chronicler presents to us another scene as a sequel to the story. A prisoner, a suspected heretic named Constantine, was being tried a few months later before Sir Thomas More. " Now Constantine," said the judge, " I would have thee to be plain with me in one thing that I shall ask, and I promise thee I will show thee favour in all other things whereof thou art accused. There

[1] " Halle's Chronicle."

are beyond the sea Tyndale, Joye, and a great many of you; I know they cannot live without help. There must be some that help and succour them with money, and thou, being one of them, hadst thy part thereof, and therefore knowest from whence it came. I pray thee, tell me who be they that help them thus."

"My lord," quoth Constantine, "I will tell thee truly—it is the Bishop of London that hath holpen us, for he hath bestowed among us a great deal of money upon New Testaments to burn them, and that hath been our chief succour and comfort."

"Now by my troth," quoth Sir Thomas More, "I think even the same, for I told the bishop thus much before he went about it."

The opponents of the book began at last to see that a printed Testament continually being produced was quite beyond their power to destroy. Bishop Tonstal profited by his lesson, and instead of buying and burning the book any longer, he preached a famous sermon at Paul's Cross, declaring its "naughtiness," and asserting that he himself had found in it more than two thousand errors; [1] and at the close of his sermon he hurled the copy which he held into a great fire that blazed before him. Sir Thomas More, whose influence was deservedly great in England, followed up the attack. "To study to find errors in Tyndale's book," he said, "were like studying to find water in the sea." It was even too bad for revising and amend-

[1] "There is not so much as one i therein," says Tyndale, "if it lack the tittle over its head, but they have noted and number it to the ignorant people for a heresy."

ing, "for it is easier to make a web of new cloth than it is to sew up every hole in a net."[1] Tyndale indignantly replied to this attack; and certainly his opponent does not show to advantage in the argument, his sweeping charge narrowing itself down at the last to the mis-translation of half a dozen words.

Such attacks, made from different pulpits throughout the land, were much more effective than the previous stupid measures adopted against the Bible, chiefly because the people could seldom hear the refutation. But this was not always so. The friends of the Refor-mation were increasing in England, and they as well as Tyndale defended the book when they could, and generally with success.

In 1529 Latimer had preached at Cambridge his celebrated sermons "On the Card," which attracted a good deal of attention, arguing in favour of the trans-lation and universal reading of Holy Scripture. The friars were enraged, and the more so as his reasoning was so difficult to answer. At length they selected a champion, Friar Buckingham; and certainly, if he may be taken as a type of the friars of his day, the Re-formers' sneers at their ignorance were not without grounds.[2] A Sunday was fixed on which he was to

---

[1] More's *animus* against Tyndale is amusingly shown in his descrip-tion of the translation of Jonah—"Jonas made out by Tyndale—a book that whoso delyte therein shall stande in peril that Jonas was never so swallowed up by the whale as by the delyte of that booke a mannes soul may be swallowed up by the Devyl that he shall never have the grace to get out again."

[2] "They said there was a new language discovered called Greek, of which people should beware, since it was that which produced all

demolish the arguments of Latimer, and on the appointed day the people assembled, and a sermon against Bible translation was preached which to us now must read more like jest than sober argument.

"Thus," asked the preacher with a triumphant smile, "where Scripture saith no man that layeth his hand to the plough and looketh back is fit for the kingdom of God, will not the ploughman when he readeth these words be apt forthwith to cease from his plough, and then where will be the sowing and the harvest? Likewise also whereas the baker readeth, 'A little leaven leaveneth the whole lump,' will he not be forthwith too sparing in the use of leaven, to the great injury of our health. And so also when the simple man reads the words, 'If thine eye offend thee pluck it out and cast it from thee,' incontinent he will pluck out his eyes, and so the whole realm will be full of blind men, to the great decay of the nation and the manifest loss of the King's grace. And thus by reading of the Holy Scriptures will the whole realm come into confusion."

The next Sunday St. Edward's Church was crowded to suffocation, for the report had gone abroad that Latimer was to reply to the Grey Friar's sermon. At the close of the prayers the old man ascended the pulpit, and amid breathless silence the sermon began—such a crushing, scathing rebuke as Buckingham and his party never recovered in Cambridge. One by one the argu-

the heresies ; that in this language was come forth the New Testament, which was full of thorns and briars ; that there was another new language too, called Hebrew, and they who learned it were turned Hebrews."—*Hody, De Textibus Bibl.*

ments were ridiculed as too foolish for a really serious reply. "Only children and fools," he said, "fail to distinguish between the figurative and the real meanings of language—between the image which is used and the thing which that image is intended to represent. For example," he continued, with a withering glance at his opponent, who sat before the pulpit, "if we paint a fox preaching in a friar's hood, nobody imagines that a fox is meant, but that craft and hypocrisy are described, which so often are found disguised in that garb."

It was evident, too, that many of the people sympathised with the Reformers in such contests. Day by day it became clearer now that the tide of public opinion in England was setting too strongly to be resisted in favour of a "People's Bible." In spite of all opposition the book was being everywhere talked about and read. "It passeth my power," writes Bishop Nikke, complaining to the Primate, "it passeth my power, or that of any spiritual man, to hinder it now, and if this continue much longer it will undo us all." There was no room for questioning about it. The path of the Bible was open at last. Not king nor pope could stay its progress now. Over England's long night of error and superstition and soul-crushing despotism God had said, "Let there be light!" and there was light.

§ 5. But the Light-bringer himself did not see that day. For weary years he had laboured for it, a worn, poverty-stricken exile in a far away German town, and now when it came his heroic life was over—the prison and the stake had done their work. His enemies were many and powerful in England, and Vaughan, the royal envoy, had been instructed to persuade him to return. But Tyndale refused to go. "Whatever promises of safety may be made," he said, "the king would never be able to protect me from the bishops, who believe that no faith should be kept with heretics." A friend of Sir Thomas More then undertook the task, and a treacherous villain named Phillips, a clergyman of very plausible manners, contrived to win the confidence of the unsuspecting exile, "for Tyndale was simple and inexpert in the wily subtleties of the world." He confided in Phillips as a friend, lent him money when he wanted it, and utterly refused to listen to his landlord's suspicions about the man. At length, their plans being ripe, Tyndale was enticed some distance from his house, seized by Phillips' lurking assistants, and hurried to the dungeons of the Castle of Vilvorden. It is pitiful to read of the poor prisoner there, in his cold and misery and rags, writing to the governor to beg "your lordship, and that by the Lord Jesus, that if I am to remain here during the winter, you will request the procureur to be kind enough to send me from my goods which he has in his possession a warmer cap, for I suffer extremely from a perpetual catarrh, which is much increased by this cell. A warmer coat also, for that which I have is very thin; also a piece of cloth to patch my leggings—my shirts too are worn out."

There was no hope of escape from the first. He

knew that the clerical influence in England was too strong against him to hope for any help in that quarter. Long ago he had said with sad foreboding, "If they burn me also, they shall do none other thing than I look for," and now his foreboding was to be realised. On Friday the 6th October 1536 he was strangled at the stake and then burnt to ashes, fervently praying with his last words, "Lord, open the King of England's eyes," a prayer which was nearer to its answer than the heroic martyr deemed.

There is no grander life in the whole annals of the Reformation than that of William Tyndale—none which comes nearer in its beautiful self-forgetfulness to His who "laid down His life for His sheep." Many a man has suffered in order that a great cause might conquer by means of himself. No such thought sullied the self-devotion of Tyndale. He issued his earlier editions of the New Testament without a name, "following the counsel of Christ which exhorteth men to do their good deeds secretly." "I assure you," said he to Vaughan, the envoy of the king, "if it would stand with the king's most gracious pleasure to grant a translation of the Scripture to be put forth among his people like as it is put forth among the subjects of the emperor here, be it the translation of whatsoever person he pleases, I shall immediately make faithful promises never to write more nor abide two days in these parts after the same, but immediately repair unto his realm, and there humbly submit myself at the feet of his royal majesty, offering my body to suffer what pain or torture, yea, what death his grace wills, so that this be obtained."

Poverty and distress and misrepresentation were his constant lot; imprisonment and death were ever staring him in the face; but "none of these things moved him, neither counted he his life dear unto him" for the accomplishment of the work which God had set him.

No higher honour could be given to any man than such a work to accomplish, and among all the heroes of the Reformation none worthier of that honour could be found than William Tyndale.

§ 6. And now a few words about the translation itself. As we have seen already, all the earlier English versions were but translations of a translation, being derived from the Vulgate or older Latin versions. Tyndale for the first time goes back to the original Hebrew and Greek,[1] though the manuscripts accessible in his time were not of much authority as compared with those used by our revisers now.

And not only did he go back to the original languages seeking for the truth, but he embodied that truth when found in so noble a translation that it has been but little improved on even to the present day. Every succeeding version is in reality little more than a revision of Tyndale's; even our present Authorised Version owes to him chiefly the ease and beauty for

---

[1] See Diagram facing the title-page. Besides Erasmus' Greek Testament, Tyndale had also before him the Latin Vulgate and Erasmus' Latin translation of the New Testament. It is said too that he used Luther's German Bible.

which it is so admired. " The peculiar genius," says Mr. Froude, " which breathes through the English Bible, the mingled tenderness and majesty, the Saxon simplicity, the grandeur, unequalled, unapproached in the attempted improvements of modern scholars—all are here, and bear the impress of the mind of one man, and that man William Tyndale."

The New Testament was the work to which he chiefly devoted himself, bringing out edition after edition as he saw anything to be improved. Of the Old Testament he translated only the Pentateuch, the Historical Books. and part of the Prophets.

The margin contains a running comment on the text, and some of the notes rather amusingly exhibit his strong anti-Papal feeling. He has a grim jest in the margin of Exod. xxxii. 35, " The Pope's bull slayeth more than Aaron's calf." On Lev. xxi. 5 he comments, "Of the heathen priests, then, our prelates took the example of their bald pates;" and where the account is given, Exod. xxxvi. 5, &c., of the forbidding the people to bring any more offerings for the building of the tabernacle, he has this note on the margin, " When will the Pope say Hoo! (hold!) and forbid an offering for the building of St. Peter's Church? And when will our spirituality say Hoo! and forbid to give them more land? Never until they have all."

Many of his quaint expressions have been altered in succeeding versions, not always, perhaps, for the better. Here are a few as specimens taken almost entirely from the New Testament :—

Gen. xxxix. 2—"And the Lorde was with Ioseph, and he was a luckie felowe."

Matt. xxvi. 30—"When they had said grace."

Mark vi. 27—"He sent forthe the hangman."

Rev. i. 10—"I was in the Sprete on a Sondaye."

Matt. xxvii. 62—"The daye that foloweth Good Fridaye."

1 Cor. xvi. 8—"I will tarry at Ephesus til Witsontyde."

Acts xiii. 15—"The rulers of the synagogue sent to them after the lecture, saying, If ye have any sermon to exhort the people, say on."

Acts xiv. 13—"Brought oxen and garlandes to the churche porche."

1 Peter v. 3—"Be not as lordes over the parrishes."

Heb. xii. 16—"Which for one breakfast sold his birthright."

Matt. iv. 24—"Holden of divers diseases and gripinges."

Matt. vi. 7—"When ye pray, bable not moche."

Matt. xv. 27—"The whelpes eat of the crommes."

Mark xii. 2—"He sent to the tenauntes a servant."

Luke xx. 9—"He lett it forthe to fermers."

The following passage from Luke ii. I have selected as a characteristic specimen of Tyndale, though perhaps not showing as well as other passages would the resemblance to our Authorised Version. Opposite is printed the corresponding portion in Wycliffe's Testament, to show the growth of the English language in the meantime :—

Specimen from Wycliffe.

_____

(LUKE ii. 1–11.)

Forsothe it was don in tho dayes, a maundement went out fro Caesar August that al the world schulde be discruyed. This first discruyinge was maad of Cyryne iustice of Cirye, and alle men wenten that thei schulde make professioun ech by him-self in to his cite. Sothly and Joseph stighede up fro Galilee of the cite of Nazareth in to Jude, in to a cite of Dauith that is clepid Bedleem, for that he was of tho house and meyne of Dauith, that he schulde knowleche with Mary with child spousid wyf to hym.

Sothly it was don whanne thei weren there the dayes weren fulfilled that she schulde bere child. And she childide her firste born sone and wlappide hym in clothis and putted hym in a cracche, for ther was not place to hym in the compyn stable.

Specimen from Tyndale.

(LUKE ii. 1–11.)

Hit folowed in thoose dayes that there wente oute a commaundment from Auguste the Emperour that all the woorlde shulde be valued. This tarynge was first executed when Syrenus was leftenaunt in Siria. And every man wente in to his awne shire toune there to be tared. And Joseph also ascended from Galile oute of a cite called Nazareth, vnto Jewry, into a cite of David which is called Bethleem, because he was of the housse and linage of David, to be tared with Mary his wedded wyfe, which was with childe. And it fortuned while they there were her tyme was come that she shulde be delyvered. And she brought forthe her first begotten sonne and wrapped hym in swaddlynge clothes, and layed hym in a manger be cause there was no roume for them within in the hostrey.

CHAPTER VII.

THE BIBLE AFTER TYNDALE'S DAYS.

§ 1. Three Years After.   § 2. Twenty Years After.
§ 3. Fifty Years More gone by.

"LORD, open the King of England's eyes!"

Pity that William Tyndale, as he gasped forth his dying prayer, could not have lifted even a little way the veil that hid from him the future of England.

§ 1. THREE YEARS AFTER.

In every parish church stands an English Bible, whose frontispiece alone is sufficient to tell of the marvellous change that has taken place in the meantime.

The design is by Holbein. In the first compartment the Almighty is seen in the clouds with outstretched arms. Two scrolls proceed out of His mouth to the right and to the left. On the former is the phrase, "The word which goeth forth from me shall not return to me empty, but shall accomplish whatsoever I will have done." The other is addressed to King Henry, who is kneeling in the distance bareheaded, with his crown lying at his feet—"I have found me a man after mine own heart, who shall fulfil all my will." Henry answers, "Thy word is a lantern unto my feet."

Immediately below is the King, seated on his throne, holding in each hand a book, on which is written "The Word of God." This he is giving to Cranmer and another bishop, who, with a group of priests, are on the right of the picture, saying, "Take this and teach;" the other, on the opposite side, he holds out to Cromwell and the lay peers, and the words are, "I make a decree that in all my kingdom men shall tremble and fear before the Living God;" while a third scroll, falling downward over his feet, speaks alike to peer and prelate—"Judge righteous judgment; turn not away your ear from the prayer of any poor man."

In the third compartment Cranmer and Cromwell are distributing the Bibles to kneeling priests and laymen, and at the bottom a preacher with a benevolent and beautiful face is addressing a crowd from a pulpit in the open air. He is apparently commencing his sermon with the words, "I exhort, therefore, that first of all supplications, prayers, thanksgivings, be made for all men, for kings"—— and at the word "kings" the people are shouting, "Vivat Rex!" children who know no Latin lisping, "God save the King!" while at the extreme left a prisoner at a jail window is joining in the cry of delight as if he too were delivered from a worse bondage.[1]

[1] This description is taken from Mr. Froude's History of England, where, however, the frontispiece is erroneously said to belong to an edition of the Coverdale Bible.

This was the so-called "GREAT BIBLE" of 1539, the first English "Authorised Version."

It was indeed a marked change that had passed over England. The Reformation was gaining ground among clergy and laity, Henry had openly broken with the Pope, and there seemed no disposition anywhere to oppose the desire for a "People's Bible."

But the opposition to William Tyndale still remained. His stern uncompromising attitude towards Papal error had made him many enemies in Church and court. His works had already been publicly condemned, and the men who had condemned him and pursued him to his death were resolved that his Bible should never be the Bible of England.

Yet this "Great Bible," the Authorised Version of the nation, was virtually Tyndale's!

This is how it came about. Already in these three years three different versions had appeared in England. In 1536, the very year after Tyndale's imprisonment, came the Bible [1] of Myles Coverdale, the man who after

---

[1] Sometimes called the "Treacle Bible," from its rendering of Jer. viii. 22, "Is there no triacle in Gilead?" Here are some other curious expressions :—

Gen. viii. 11—"The dove bare an olive leafe in her nebbe."

Joshua ii. 11—"Our heart had fayled us, neither is there good stomacke in any manne."

Judges ix. 53—"And brake his brain-panne."

Job v. 7—"It is man that is born to misery like as a byrd for to flee."

Acts xi. 8—"Ther widowes were not looked vpon in the daylie handreaching."

In original edition Queen Anne is referred to as the king's "dearest

Tyndale has played the most prominent part of any in the history of the English Bible. Coverdale was a man of very different stamp from his great predecessor. He had neither his ability nor strength of character, nor was he, like him, fitted by a lifelong study for his task as a translator, and the difference comes markedly out in the work produced by each. But it is only fair to say, too, that he was quite conscious of his defects, that he did the work before him to the best of his ability, "seeking it not, neither desiring it," but feeling that his country needed it done, and modestly regretting that no better man was there to do it.

His Bible makes no pretence to be an original translation; it is "translated out of Douche and Latin into English," with the help of "five sundry interpreters" (*i.e.*, translators), and the chief of these "interpreters" is evidently William Tyndale, whom, in the New Testament especially, he closely follows.

The following year (1537) appeared "Matthews' Bible,"[1] which was really prepared by John Rogers, one of the early Reformers, afterwards martyred in Queen Mary's reign. His known opinions and his connection with Tyndale accounts for the suppression of his real name as likely to injure the circulation of the book. This work was Tyndale's translation pure

juste wyfe and most virtuous princesse." A copy now in the British Museum has this inscription, but "Ane" is changed to Jane, thus JAne. The other copies have, some Ane, some Jane, while some actually leave the space blank, as if the editor were unable to keep pace with Henry's rapid change of wives.

[1] In it the Song of Solomon is entitled " 𝕾𝖔𝖑𝖔𝖒𝖔𝖓'𝖘 𝖅𝖆𝖑𝖆𝖉𝖊𝖘."

and simple, all but the latter half of the Old Testament (which is taken, with some alteration, from Coverdale's Bible); and one feels pleased for the old exile's sake, though his honour was given to others, that Archbishop Cranmer should "like it better than any translation heretofore made," he "would rather see it licensed by the king than receive £1000," and "if they waited till the bishops should set forth a better translation they would wait," he thinks, "till the day after doomsday."[1] It is not easy to understand how it escaped detection as the work of Tyndale, especially as it contained those strong anti-Papal notes by which Tyndale's version gave such offence.

Shortly after appeared "Taverner's Bible,"[2] which was little more than an edition of Matthews' with its more violent polemical notes toned down or omitted.

None of these versions were satisfactory. Coverdale's was but a second-hand translation, and Matthews' was only in part derived from the originals, besides which the controversial notes were against its success.

So it came to pass that the Great Bible was set on

---

[1] "Cranmer's Remains and Letters," p. 344. Parker Society.

[2] Little is known of him. The description in Fuller's "Church History," chap. ii. p. 459, is certainly not flattering—"Surely preaching must have run very low if it be true what I read that Mr. Tavernour of Water Eaton, in Oxfordshire, gave the scholars a sermon at St. Mary's with his gold chain about his neck and his sword by his side, beginning with these words, 'Arriving at Mount St. Mary's, in the stony stage where I now stand, I have brought you some fine biscuits baked in the oven of charity and carefully conserved for the chickens of the Church, the sparrows of the Spirit, the sweet swallows of salvation.'"

12898

foot. Cranmer and some of the chief advisers of the
king had set their hearts on having a translation that
would be really worthy of its position as a National
Bible. Myles Coverdale was selected to take charge
of the work, and he proceeded to Paris with the king's
printer, that the book might be brought out in the best
possible style. But the Inquisitor-General got notice
of the project, and the result was a repetition of the
episode of Tyndale at Cologne, only that Coverdale
fared better than his great predecessor, for though his
Bibles were all seized by the "Lieutenant Criminall,"
he carried off the printing-press, the types, and the
printers themselves to complete the work in England.
It was published in April 1539, and was "authorised to
be used and frequented in every church in the kingdom."[1] The reader who wants a specimen of its style
has but to turn to the Psalms in his Prayer-Book or
the "Comfortable Words" in the Communion Service,
which are taken unchanged from the Great Bible. It
has another point of interest in connection with the
Revised Version. It indicated some texts as doubtful
by printing them in small type, and among them was
the celebrated passage 1 John v. 7, 8, which the recent
revisers have omitted altogether.

But more important to notice is the fact that the
book is really no new translation. It may be described

---

[1] When Henry was asked to authorise it, "Well," said he, "but are
there any heresies maintained thereby?" They answered that there
were no heresies that they could find maintained in it. "Then in
God's name," said the king, "let it go forth among our people."

as a compilation from Matthews' and Coverdale's Bibles
—or better still, perhaps, with a recent writer,[1] as a
revision of Matthews' by Coverdale; and since, as we
have seen, Matthews' was almost entirely Tyndale's
version, the Great Bible was really little more than a
revised edition of Tyndale!

Thus had the old martyr triumphed. Only three
years since these men had brought him to his death,
and here was his Bible in their midst, though they
knew it not, authorised by the king, commended by
the clergy, and placed in the parish churches for the
teaching of the people! And as if to mark the change
with all the emphasis that was possible, an inscription
on the title-page told that "it was oversene and perused
at the commandement of the King's Highness by the
ryghte reverende fathers in God, Cuthbert bishop of
Duresme (Durham), and Nicholas bishop of Rochester."
Who, think you, reader, was Cuthbert of Duresme?
None other than Cuthbert Tonstal, his untiring opponent, the bishop who had turned him discouraged from
his door, who had bargained with Pakington to pur-
chase the Bibles, who had hurled into the flames from
the pulpit of Paul's Cross the translation which now
went forth bearing his name!

§ 2. Twenty Years After.

It is the day of Elizabeth's entry into London, and
the streets are bright with waving banners and gay
dresses of the citizens struggling to get closer to the

---

[1] Dr. Mombert, "English Versions."

royal procession, and shouting with joy as they behold their young queen. There is more in those shouts than the mere gaiety of a holiday crowd. It is a glad day for many in England. The dark reign of Mary is over, with its imprisonments and martyrdoms, and the men of the Reformation are looking forward hopefully to the future. There are those in that crowd who have lived for years in constant dread—there are those who have had to fly for their lives, some of them companions of the exiles at Geneva, waiting to send word to their comrades abroad how it should fare in England.

Now the shouting has ceased. There is a pause in the long line of banners and plumes and glittering steel. The procession has just arrived at "the Little Conduit in Chepe," where one of those pageants, the delight of our forefathers, is prepared. An old man in emblematic dress stands forth before the queen, and it is told Her Grace that this is Time. "Time," quoth she, "and Time it was that brought me hither." Beside him stands a white-robed maiden, who is introduced as "Truth, the daughter of Time." She holds in her hand a book on which is written, " *Verbum veritatis*," the Word of truth, an English Bible, which she presents to the queen. Raising it with both her hands, Elizabeth presses it to her lips, and then laying it against her heart, amid the enthusiastic shouting of the multitude, she gracefully thanks the city for so precious a gift.

It was a good omen for the future of the Bible, which had been almost a closed book in the preceding reign. And within three months it was followed by one still more significant. The Reformers who had fled to Geneva returned to their homes, bearing with them a new version of the Bible, the work of the best years of their banishment,[1] and the dedication of the book was accepted by Elizabeth.

This was the first appearance in England of the famous Geneva Bible, the "Breeches Bible," as it was afterwards called, from its rendering of Genesis iii. 7, where Adam and Eve "sewed fig-tree leaves together, and made themselves breeches."[2] It was the most popular Bible that had ever appeared in England, and for sixty years it held its own against all rivals, for a time contesting the ground even with our own Authorised Version.

It was both cheaper and less cumbrous than the "Great Bible" of Cranmer, as well as being a much more careful and accurate work, though, like most of its predecessors, it was more a revision than a translation, being chiefly based on Tyndale. It contained marginal notes, which were considered very helpful in dealing with obscure passages of Scripture,[3] though, as might

---

[1] Myles Coverdale was one of them.

[2] It was really only one edition published by Barker that contained this reading, which was also the reading of Wycliffe's Bible.

[3] I do not know if the note on Rev. ix. 3 would be thus classed. The "locusts that came out of the bottomless pit" are explained as meaning "false teachers, heretics, and worldly subtil prelates, with Monks, Friars, Cardinals, Patriarchs, Archbishops, Bishops, Doctors, Bachelors and Masters of Artes, which forsake Christ to maintain false doctrine."

be expected from Geneva, of a strongly Calvinistic bias. These notes should possess a special interest for us, for, as we shall see afterward, we have partly to thank them for our Authorised Version of to-day.

Some other of its peculiarities are worth notice. It was the first Bible that laid aside the old black letter for the present Roman type. It was also the first to recognise the divisions into verses, and the first to omit the Apocrypha. It omits the name of St. Paul from the Epistle to the Hebrews, and it uses italics for all words not occurring in the original.

The history of the dark troublous days of opposition to the Bible and persecution to its promoters ceases for ever (let us hope) with the issue of the Geneva Bible.

§ 3. FIFTY YEARS MORE GONE BY.

How Tyndale's heart would have swelled at the sight! A king of England himself is directing an English Bible translation!

In January 1604 a conference of bishops and clergy had been held in the drawing-rooms of Hampton Court Palace, under the presidency of King James himself, to consider certain alleged grievances of the Puritan party in the Church, and among other subjects of discussion was rather unexpectedly brought up that of the defectiveness of the two current translations of Scripture.

Specimens.

23D PSALM.

COVERDALE'S, 1535.   GREAT BIBLE, 1539.

The Lorde is my shepherde I can want nothing. He fedeth me in a greene pasture and ledeth me to a fresh water. He quickeneth my soule and bringeth me forth in the waye of righteeousnes for his names sake. Though I shulde walke now in the balley of the shadowe of death yet I feare no euell for thou art with me, thy staffe and thy shepehoke comforte me.

Thou preparest a table before agaynst mine enemies thou anoyntest my heade with oyle and fyllest my cuppe full. Oh let thy louing-kyndnes and mercy folowe me all the dayes off my lyfe that I maye dwell in the house off the Lord for euer.

The Lorde is my shepherde therefore can I lacke nothing. He shal fede me in a grene pasture and leade me forth besyde ye watirs of coforte. He shal conuert my soule and bring me forth in ye pathes of righteousnes for his names sake. Yea though I walke thorowe ye balleye of ye shadowe of death I wyl fear no euell for thou art wt me: thy rod and thy staffe comfort me.

Thou shalt prepare a table before me agaynst them that trouble me: thou has anoynted my head wt oyle and my cup shal be ful. But louing kyndnes and mercy shal folowe me all the dayes of my lyfe and I wyll dwel in ye house of ye Lorde for euer.

England had at that time three different versions. The Genevan was the favourite of the people in general; a rival version, called the Bishops' Bible, which had been brought out some eight years after, was supported

Specimens.

23D PSALM.

GENEVAN BIBLE, 1560.

1. The Lord *is* my shepheard I shall not want.

2. Hee maketh mee to rest in greene pasture *and* leadeth mee by the still waters.

3. He restoreth my soule *and* leadeth me in the paths of righteousnesse for His Names sake.

4. Ye though I walk through the valley of the shadowe of death I will feare no euill for thou art with me : thy rodde and thy staffe they comfort me.

5. Thou doest prepare a table before me in the sight of mine adversaries ; thou dost anoynt mine head with oyle *and* my cup runneth over.

6. Doubtlesse kindnesse and mercy shall follow mee all the dayes of my life and I shal remaine a long season in the house of the Lord.

BISHOPS' BIBLE, 1568.

1. God is my shephearde therefore I can lacke nothyng : he wyll cause me to repose my-selfe in pasture full of grasse and he wyll leade me vnto calme waters.

2. He will conuert my soule ; he wyll bring me foorth into the pathes of righteousnesse for his names sake.

3. Yea though I walke through the valley of the shadowe of death I wyll fear no euyll ; for thou art with me, thy rodde and thy staffe be the thynges that do comfort me.

4. Thou wilt prepare a table before me in the presence of myne aduersaries ; thou has anoynted my head with oyle and my cup shalbe brymme ful.

5. Truly felicitie and mercy shal folowe me all the dayes of my lyfe : and I wyll dwell in the house of God for a long tyme.

by ecclesiastical authority ; while the " Great Bible " of Henry VIII. might still be seen chained to a stone or wooden desk in many of the country churches. But none of these was likely to be accepted as the Bible of the English nation. The Great Bible was antiquated and cumbersome, the Genevan, though a careful translation and convenient for general use, had become, through the Puritan character of its notes, quite the Bible of a party; while the Bishops' Version, a very inferior production, neither commanded the respect of scholars nor suited the wants of the people.

There was, therefore, plainly a need for a new version, which, being accepted by all, should form a bond of union between different classes and rival religious communities. Yet when Dr. Reynolds, the leader of the Puritan party, put forward such a proposal at the Conference, it was very coldly received, Bancroft, bishop of London, seeming to express the general feeling of his party when he grumbled that "if every man had his humour about new versions, there would be no end of translating." Probably the fact of the proposal having come from the Puritans had also some effect on this conservatism of the bishops; in any case it seemed that the project must fall through for want of their support.

But if the bishops in the palace drawing-room that day thought so, they soon found that they had literally "calculated without their host." There was one man in that assembly who looked with special favour on the new proposal, and that man was the royal pedant who presided. A Bible translation made under his auspices would greatly add to the glory of his reign, besides which, to a man whose learning was really considerable, and who was specially fond of displaying it in theological matters, the direction of such a work would be very congenial. And if a further motive were needed, it was easily found in his unconcealed dislike to the popular Geneva Bible. The whole tone of its politics and theology, as exhibited in the marginal notes, was utterly distasteful to James, as he plainly showed soon after in his directions to the new translators, for " marry withal, he gave this caveat, that no notes should be added, having found in those which were annexed to the Geneva translation some notes very partial, untrue, seditious, and savouring too much of dangerous and traitorous conceits."

Two of these notes especially vexed him. In 2 Chron. xv. 16 it is recorded that Asa " removed his mother from being queen, because she had made an idol in a grove ;" and the margin contains this comment, " Herein he showed that he lacked zeal, for she ought to have died," a remark probably often remembered by the fanatics of the day in reference to the death of James's mother, the Queen of Scots. There was another which rather amusingly clashed with the grand Stuart theories of the divine right of kings to be above all law and to command implicit obedience from their subjects. In the passage in the first chapter of Exodus describing the conduct of the Hebrew midwives, who " did not as the king of Egypt commanded, but saved the men-children alive," the margin declares " their disobedience to the king was lawful, though their dissembling was evil." " It is false," cried the indignant advocate of kingly right ; " to disobey a king is not lawful ; such traitorous conceits should not go forth among the people."

But, however men may smile at the absurdities of James, which in some measure led to the new translation, there can be no question as to the wisdom shown in his arrangements for carrying out the work. Fifty-four learned men were selected impartially from High Churchmen and Puritans, as well as from those who, like Saville and Boys, represented scholarship totally unconnected with any party. And in addition to this band of appointed revisers, the king also designed to secure the co-operation of every Biblical scholar of note in the kingdom. The Vice-Chancellor of Cambridge was desired to name any fit man with whom he was acquainted, and Bishop Bancroft received a letter from the king himself, directing him to "move the bishops to inform themselves of all such learned men within their several dioceses as, having especial skill in the Hebrew and Greek tongues, have taken pains in their private studies of the Scriptures for the clearing of any obscurities either in the Hebrew or the Greek, or touching any difficulties or mistakings in the former English translations, which we have now commanded to be thoroughly viewed and amended, and thereupon to earnestly charge them, signifying our pleasure therein, that they send such their observations to Mr. Lively, our Hebrew reader in Cambridge, or to Dr. Harding, our Hebrew reader in Oxford, or to Dr. Andrews, Dean of Westminster, to be imparted to the rest of their several companies, that so our said intended translation may have the help and furtherance of all our principal learned men within this our kingdom."

An admirable set of rules was drawn up for the instruction of the revisers, directing amongst other things that the Bishops' Bible should be used as a basis, and departed from only when the text required it; that any competent scholars might be consulted about special difficulties; that differences of opinion should be settled at a general meeting; that divisions of chapters should be as little changed as possible, and marginal references should be given from one scripture to another; and last, but by no means least, that there should be no marginal notes, except for the explanation of Hebrew and Greek words. This simple rule did probably more than anything else to make our Authorised Version the Bible of all classes in England, binding us together as a Protestant nation by a tie which the strife of parties and the war of politics has since been insufficient to sever. Had the opposite course been adopted, we should now have probably the Bibles of different religious parties competing in unseemly rivalry, each reflecting the theological bias of the party from which it came.

Never before had such labour and care been expended on the English Bible. The revisers were divided into six companies, each of which took its own portion, and every aid accessible was used to make their work a thorough success. They carefully studied the Greek and Hebrew; they used the best commentaries of European scholars; the Bibles in Spanish, Italian, French, and German were examined for any help they might afford in arriving at the exact sense of each passage; and when the sense was found, no pains were spared to express it in clear, vigorous, idiomatic English. All the excellences of the previous versions were noted, for the purpose of incorporating them in the work, and even the Rhemish (Roman Catholic) translation was laid under contribution for some expressive phrases which it contained. " Neither," says Dr. Miles Smith, in the preface, " did we disdain to revise that which we had done, and to bring back to the anvil that which we had hammered, fearing no reproach for slowness nor coveting praise for expedition;" and the result was the production of this splendid Authorised Version of which Englishmen to-day are so justly proud.

For more than two centuries English Protestant writers have spoken of it in terms of almost unanimous praise—its " grace and dignity," its " flowing words," its " masterly English style." Even a Roman Catholic divine, Dr. Geddes (1786), declares that "if accuracy and strictest attention to the letter of the text be supposed to constitute an excellent version, this is of all versions the most excellent." And an almost touching tribute is paid it by one who evidently looked back on it with yearning regret, after having exchanged its beauties for the uncouthness of the Romanist versions. " Who will say," writes Father Faber, " that the uncommon beauty and marvellous English of the Protestant Bible is not one of the great strongholds of heresy in this country? It lives on the ear like a music that can never be forgotten,

like the sound of church bells, which the convert
scarcely knows how he can forego. Its felicities seem
often to be almost things rather than words. It is
part of the national mind, and the anchor of the
national seriousness. Nay, it is worshipped with a
positive idolatry, in extenuation of whose fanaticism
its intrinsic beauty pleads availingly with the scholar.
The memory of the dead passes into it. The potent
traditions of childhood are stereotyped in its verses.
It is the representative of a man's best moments; all
that there has been about him of soft, and gentle, and
pure, and penitent, and good speaks to him for ever
out of his English Bible. It is his sacred thing,
which doubt never dimmed and controversy never
soiled; and in the length and breadth of the land there
is not a Protestant with one spark of religiousness
about him whose spiritual biography is not in his
Saxon Bible."

CHAPTER VIII.

THE REVISED VERSION.

§ 1. Preparation for Revision. § 2. The Jerusalem Chamber. § 3. The Revisers at Work. § 4. Claims of the Revised Bible. § 5. Will it Disturb Men's Faith? § 6. General Remarks—Conclusion.

WHILE fully appreciating the beauty and excellence of his Authorised Version, the reader who has thus far followed this little sketch will scarcely require now to ask, Why should we need a new revision?

He will have seen that the whole history of the Bible from Tyndale's days is a history of growth and improvement by means of repeated revisions. Tyndale's first New Testament (1525) was revised by himself in 1534, and again in 1535. In Matthews' Bible it appeared still more improved in 1537. The Great Bible (1539) was the result of a further revision, which was repeated again in the Genevan (1560), the Bishops' (1568), and still more thoroughly in our splendid Authorised Version (1611), which latter is itself one of the best proofs of the value of Bible revision.

He will have seen also (to recapitulate here for

greater clearness)—(1.) that in the present day we have access to a treasury of ancient manuscripts, versions, and quotations such as the scholars of King James's day had never dreamed of; (2.) that the science of textual criticism, which teaches the value and the best methods of dealing with these documents, has entirely sprung up since; (3.) that our scholars are better acquainted with the Sacred Languages, and able to distinguish delicate shades of meaning which were quite lost on their predecessors; and (4.) lastly, that owing to the natural growth of the English language itself many words in the Authorised Version have become obsolete, and several have completely changed their meaning during the past 300 years.

And thus the duty is laid upon our Biblical scholars which Tyndale in his first preface imposed on those of his own day, " that if they perceive in any place that the version has not attained unto the very sense of the tongue or the very meaning of Scripture, or have not given the right English word, that they should put to their hands and amend it, *remembering that so is their duty to do.*"

About the beginning of the present century the appearance of several partial revisions by private individuals indicated the feeling in the minds of scholars that the time for a new Bible Revision was at hand. As years went on the feeling grew stronger, and leading men in the Church were pleading that the work should not be long delayed. During the past

H

250 years, they urged, great stores of Biblical information have been accumulating;[1] our ability to use such
information has been greatly increased; and it is of
importance to the interests of religion that that information should be fully disseminated by a careful correction of our received Scriptures.   Dr. Tischendorf's
discovery at Mount Sinai still further intensified this
feeling; and so it created little surprise when, on the
10th February 1870, Bishop Wilberforce rose in the
Upper House of the Southern Convocation to propose,
"That a committee of both Houses be appointed, with
power to confer with any committee that may be
appointed by the Convocation of the Northern Province,
to report on the desirableness of a revision of the
Authorised Version of the New Testament, whether
by marginal notes or otherwise, in all those passages
where plain and clear errors, whether in the Greek
text adopted by the translators, or in the translation

[1] Fully 200 years ago the way began to be prepared for our present revision by several criticisms and attempts at correction of the
Authorised Version.   It soon became clear, however, that such attempts
were premature in the then state of information as to the Original
Scriptures, and scholars began to direct their attention rather to the
laying of the foundation for a revision in the future by collecting and
examining Greek and Hebrew manuscripts, together with the various
early versions and quotations from the Fathers.   Towards the close of
the eighteenth century Kennicott and De Rossi had published the
results of their examination of several hundred Hebrew manuscripts;
and in more recent times the same service was rendered to the Greek
by Drs. Tischendorf, Tregelles, Scrivener, and others, whose way had
been prepared by many distinguished predecessors.   Besides, there was
the work of a long series of commentators in investigating the meaning
of the Sacred Writers, so that, on the whole, a very valuable foundation for revision existed by the middle of the present century.

made from the same, shall on due investigation be
found to exist." After the enlarging of this resolution
so as to include the Old Testament also, it was adopted
by both Houses.

§ 2. Four months later, on a bright summer day
towards the close of June 1870, a distinguished
company was assembled in the Jerusalem Chamber
in Westminster Abbey.

In that room in days long gone by the first of the
Lancastrian kings breathed out his weary life. Beneath
those windows sat the "Assembly of Divines" when
the ill-fated Charles ruled in England ; here the Westminster Confession was drawn up ; and here too, under
the auspices of William of Orange, was discussed the
great Prayer-Book Revision of 1689, intended to join
together Churchmen and Dissenters.

But no memory of that ancient chamber will eclipse
in the future that of the work for which these men
were assembled on that summer afternoon, for the
Bible Revision had at length been begun, and this was
the appointed New Testament Company.

At the centre of the long table sat the chairman,
Bishop Ellicott, and around him the flower of our
English scholarship. There were Alford and Stanley
and Lightfoot, intently studying the sheets before them
on the table. Westcott was there, and Hort and
Scrivener—names long famous in the history of textual
criticism—Dr. Eadie of Scotland, and the Master of
the Temple, and the venerable Archbishop Trench of

Dublin, with many other scholars no less distinguished than they. Different religious communities were represented—different schools of thought—different opinions on matters closely connected with the work in hand. This is one of the great securities for the fairness of the New Revision. Whatever other charges may be brought against it, that of bias, even unconscious bias, towards any set of theological views is quite out of the question where Baptist and Methodist and Presbyterian and Churchman sat side by side in the selected company of Revisers. And, as if to make this assurance doubly sure, across the Atlantic a similarly constituted company was preparing to co-operate with these to criticise the work and suggest emendations, so that on the whole nearly a hundred of the ripest scholars of England and America were connected with the New Revision.

§ 3. And now let us watch the Revisers at their work. Before each man lies a sheet with a column of the Authorised Version printed in the middle, leaving a wide margin on either side for suggested alterations, the left hand for changes in the Greek text, and the right for those referring to the English rendering. These sheets are already covered with notes, the result of each Reviser's private study of the passage beforehand. After prayers and reading of the minutes, the chairman reads over for the company part of the passage on the printed sheet (Matt. i. 18–25), and asks for any suggested emendations.

At the first verse a member, referring to the notes on his sheet, remarks that certain old manuscripts read " the birth of the Christ " instead of " the birth of Jesus Christ." Dr. Scrivener and Dr. Hort state the evidence on the subject, and after a full discussion it is decided by the votes of the meeting that the received reading has most authority in its favour ; but, in order to represent fairly the state of the case, it is allowed that the margin should contain the words, " Some ancient authorities read ' of the Christ.' " Some of the members are of opinion that the name " Holy Ghost " in same verse would be better if modernised into " Holy Spirit," but as this is a mere question of rendering, it is laid aside until the textual corrections have been discussed. The next of importance is the word " first-born " in ver. 25, which is omitted in many old authorities. Again the evidence on both sides is fully stated, and the members present, each of whom has already privately studied it before, vote on the question, the result being that the words " her first-born " are omitted.

And now, the textual question being settled, the chairman asks for suggestions as to the rendering, and it is proposed that in the first verse the word " betrothed " should be substituted for " espoused," the latter being rather an antiquated form. This also is decided by vote in the affirmative, and thus they proceed verse by verse till the close of the meeting, when the whole passage, as amended, is read over by the chairman.

Four years afterward we glance at their work again.

They have reached now the First Epistle General of St. John, and the sheets lying before them contain part of the 5th chapter. No question of importance arises till the 7th verse is reached—

7. "For there are three that bear record [in heaven—the Father, the Word, and the Holy Ghost, and these three are one.

8. And there are three that bear witness in earth], the Spirit, and the Water, and the Blood, and these three agree in one"—

when it is proposed that that part of the passage which we have here placed in brackets be omitted as not belonging to the original text.

Time was when such a suggestion would have roused a formidable controversy;[1] but textual criticism has greatly progressed since then, and the question is not considered by the Revisers even to need discussing. The evidence is as follows:—The passage occurs in two *modern* Greek manuscripts—one of them in the library of Trinity College, Dublin—in one or two Ancient Versions of comparatively little value, and many modern copies of the Vulgate; besides which it is quoted by a few African Fathers, whose testimony, on the whole, is not of much weight in its favour.

Against this are to be set the following facts:— (1.) Not a single Greek manuscript or church lesson-book before the fifteenth century has any trace of the passage. This in itself would be sufficient evidence against it.   (2.) It is omitted in almost every Ancient Version of any critical value, including the best copies

---

[1] Upwards of fifty books, pamphlets, &c., written on the subject are mentioned in Horne's Introduction.

of the Vulgate (St. Jerome's Revised Bible); and (3.) no Greek Father quotes it even in the arguments about the Trinity, where it would have been of immense importance if it had been in their copies. There is other evidence against it also; but it must be quite clear, even from this, that the passage only lately got interpolated into our Greek Testament, and never had any right to its place in the English Bible.[1] The Revisers therefore omit it from the text.

But the reader must not think that this description represents the amount of care bestowed on the work. After this first revision had been completed, of a certain portion, it was transmitted to America and reviewed by the American committee, and returned again to England. Then it underwent a second revision, taking into account the American suggestions, and was again sent back to America to be reviewed. After these four revisions it underwent a fifth in England, chiefly with a view of removing any roughness of rendering. And there was yet a sixth, and in some cases even a seventh revision, for the

---

[1] Erasmus (see page 76), not finding the words in any Greek manuscript, omitted them from the first two editions of his Greek Testament, which was chiefly the authority that our translators used. But as they had long stood in the Latin Vulgate, an outcry was at once raised that he was tampering with the Bible. He insisted that no Greek manuscript contained the passage; "and," said he at last, when they pressed him, "if you can show me even a single one in which they occur, I will insert them in the future." Unfortunately they did find one, the manuscript of Montfort, which is now in the library of Trinity College, Dublin, but is evidently no older than about the fifteenth century. The words had got into it probably from some corrupt Latin manuscript; and on this slight authority Erasmus admitted them into his text.

settling of points that we need not enter on more fully here. So that we may have every confidence that the changes made, whatever their merits, at least were made only after the most thorough consideration.

And so the work went on, month after month, and more than ten years had passed, and some of the most eminent of those who sat that summer day in the Jerusalem Chamber were numbered among the dead, when, on the evening of November 11, 1880, the New Testament Company assembled in the church of St. Martin-in-Fields for a special service of prayer and thanksgiving—" of thanksgiving for the happy completion of their labours—of prayer that all that had been wrong in their spirit or action might mercifully be forgiven, and that He whose glory they had humbly striven to promote might graciously accept this their service, and use it for the good of man and the honour of His holy Name."

Four years afterwards the Old Testament Company finished their work, and on May 5th, 1885, the complete Revised Bible was in the hands of the public.

§ 4. And now a few words about this Revised Bible. It is quite outside the plan of this little book to offer any criticisms on its merits or demerits, or any judgment as to its ultimate reception. Indeed, it is rather soon yet to pronounce very confidently on either question. For many years after its first appearance our present grand Old Version had to encounter fierce opposition and severe criticism——Broughton, the greatest Hebrew scholar of the day, wrote to King James that he " would rather be torn asunder by wild horses than allow such a version to be imposed on the Church," [1]——and yet in the end it won its way and attained a position that no version before or since in any country has attained.

Whether the New Version will equally succeed, or whether, as is the general opinion, it will need a revision before being fully received, remains yet to be seen. But in any case let us give it a fair unprejudiced reception. Dr. Bickersteth tells of a smart young American deacon who thought to crush it on its first appearance by informing his people that " if the Authorised Version was good enough for St. Paul it was good enough for him," and it is to be feared that with many people who are far less ignorant there is sometimes a similar spirit exhibited.

Now let us remember that, whatever the merits or demerits of the book, it is at least entitled to respect as an earnest attempt to get nearer to the truth, and to present to English-speaking people the results of two centuries of study by the most eminent Biblical scholars.

And remember, too, that no previous revision has ever had such advantages as this. Not to speak of the

---

[1] In fifteen verses of Luke iii., he says, the translators have fifteen score of idle words to account for in the Day of Judgment. With Archbishop Bancroft, who took the lead in the work, he is especially indignant. He believes that by-and-by King James, looking down from Abraham's bosom, shall behold Bancroft in the place of torment.

valuable manuscripts available, " upon no previous
revision have so many scholars been engaged. In no
previous revision has the co-operation of those engaged
on it been so equally diffused over all parts of the
work. In no previous revision have those who took
the lead in it shown so large a measure of Christian
confidence in those who were outside their own communion. In no previous revision have such effective
precautions been created by the very composition of
the body of Revisers against accidental oversight or
against any lurking bias that might arise from natural
tendencies or ecclesiastical prepossessions. On these
accounts alone, if on no other, this Revision may be
fairly said to possess peculiar claims upon the confidence of all thoughtful and devout readers of the
Bible."

§ 5. It was objected by some, when this Revision
was first proposed, that it would be dangerous to un-
settle men's faith by showing them that the old Bible
they so reverenced contained many passages wrongly
translated, and some even which had no right to a
place in it at all. It is pleasant to see that such un-
worthy sentiments are rapidly disappearing. It would
be a sad case indeed if men's faith were to depend
on their teachers keeping from them facts which they
themselves have long since known—acting, to use
Dean Stanley's scathing comparison, like the Greek
bishops at Jerusalem, who pretend at Easter to receive
the sacred fire from heaven, and though they do not

profess to believe personally in the supposed miracle, yet retain the ceremonial, lest the ignorant multitudes who believe in it should have their minds disquieted.

Far better to do what has been done—fearlessly make any changes that were necessary to remove the few superficial flaws in our Bible, and try to teach men the grounds on which such changes were made. Our faith is given to the infallible words of the inspired writers. It is no disparagement to them if we discover that fallible men in collecting and translating these words have sometimes made mistakes, and it is certainly no honour to the words which we profess to reverence if we knowingly allow these mistakes to remain uncorrected.

When King James's translation was offered there was no such fear of unsettling men's faith, for the men of that day had already four or five different Bibles competing for their favour, and so they easily distinguished between an Inspired Original and the English versions of that original, one of which might easily be better than another.

Rightly understood, this Revision should be rather a ground for increased confidence, showing us how nearly perfect we may consider our English Bible already, when we find that this thorough criticism and the investigation of material collecting for the past two hundred years has left unchanged every doctrine which we found in our Old Version, while it certainly is helping us to understand some of them more clearly than we ever did before.

§ 6. A few remarks on the New Revision itself will close this chapter. The Revisers refer to their work under the heads of TEXT, TRANSLATION, LANGUAGE, and MARGINAL NOTES.

Whatever may be thought of their corrections of the TEXT (*i.e.*, the original Hebrew and Greek), the reader is already in a position in some measure to judge of the sources of information accessible to them and of their fitness to make such corrections.

As to TRANSLATION and LANGUAGE, perhaps there is foundation for the charge against the New Testament Company at least, of having disregarded the first rule laid down for them by Convocation, "to introduce as few alterations as possible into the text of the Authorised Version." But before condemning them it is only fair to read their explanations in the Preface. This at least will be universally allowed, that if we have lost in smoothness and beauty of diction, we have greatly gained in point of accuracy. A scrupulous attention to the force of the Greek article, the different tenses of verbs, and the delicate shades of meaning in particles and prepositions, will account for many of the minor changes, which, though they may seem at first sight trifling and unnecessary, will often be found to affect seriously the meaning of a passage. The Revisers also claim to have avoided the practice, adopted in the Authorised Version, of translating for the sake of euphony the same Greek word by different English words. For example, we have comforter and advocate—eternal and everlasting—count, and impute, and reckon [1]—as respectively renderings of the same Greek word, while, on the other hand, to take only one example, the word "ordain" represents ten different words in the original Greek. The result of such a practice is, that the English reader, using a Concordance or the marginal references of his Bible to compare passages where the same word occurs, is sometimes misled and frequently loses much useful information.

In such cases the Revisers have sacrificed elegance to accuracy of translation, though, of course, that is not a sufficient plea, unless it can be shown that elegance and accuracy cannot here go together.

The MARGINAL NOTES contain much valuable information, and often throw fresh light on the translation in the text. But it is to be regretted that in a book intended for indiscriminate circulation the Revisers have used one class of these notes rather unguardedly. When such expressions are found as "Some manuscripts read the passage thus," "Some ancient authorities omit these words," &c., the reader who understands the state of the case sees nothing disturbing in the fact that out of a large number of authorities examined some few should vary from the reading found in all the others. Such readers the Revisers seem to have had in view. They

---

[1] In Rom. iv., Authorised Version, these three verbs are used to represent one Greek verb. Let the reader turn to the Revised Version, where the word "reckon" is used throughout the chapter, and he will see how much St. Paul's argument has gained in clearness, though perhaps the passage in reading does not sound quite as well as before.

did not enough think themselves into the position of the plain simple men and women who have never heard of such matters, and on whom one cannot help fearing, from the frequent repetition of such notes, a disturbing effect which is in reality quite unwarranted.

A very valuable improvement is the arrangement of the text into paragraphs adapted to the subject. The continuity of thought is not, as in our Authorised Version, interrupted by frequent and often very injudicious breaks into verses, while yet the facilities for reference are retained by the numbering of the old division in the margin. The printing of the Poetical Books in proper metrical form may be considered, too, a decided advantage. They were directed also to revise the headings of chapters, and it would certainly be an advantage if this were well done, adapting it to the paragraph system. But there is much force in their reason for leaving it undone. It involved in many cases expressions of theological opinion which could not fairly find a place in the Bible. Indeed, Jewish readers have had to complain of the Old Testament chapter headings in the Authorised Version, that when the prophets speak of sin it is always the sin of the Jews, but when of glory and of holiness, it is the glory and holiness of the Church.

On the whole, whatever the imperfections of the Revised Bible, and whatever its fate may be in the future, we may at the very least claim a present position for it as a most valuable commentary to the readers of the Authorised Version, placing them as nearly as an English version can do on a level with the reader of the original tongues.

And now we have followed the story of the Bible from the old record chest of Ephesus 1800 years ago to the new book which is in our hands to-day, and it is hoped that the question has been in some measure answered, How we got our Bible.

Let the story help us to value our Bible more. It is not without purpose that God has so wonderfully preserved His message; it is not without purpose that He raised up His workers to search out the precious manuscripts from the dusty libraries of convent and cathedral, to collect and compare them together with such toil and care, and then to render into clear graceful English for us the very message which He sent to earth thousands of years since to comfort and brighten human life. "Other men indeed have laboured, and we have entered into their labours."

May it please Him who has so preserved for us His Word to grant us all "increase of grace to hear meekly that Word, and to receive it with pure affection, and to bring forth the fruits of the Spirit"!

THE END.

NEW WORK BY THE SAME AUTHOR.

Crown 8vo, pp. 222.—Cloth, 2s. 6d.

HOW GOD INSPIRED THE BIBLE.

Thoughts for the Present Disquiet.

ALSO,

TENTH THOUSAND. 216 pp., Cloth extra, 2s. 6d.

WITH ELEVEN ILLUSTRATIONS.

THE OLD DOCUMENTS

AND

THE NEW BIBLE.

An Easy Lesson for the People in Biblical Criticism.

DUBLIN: EASON & SON, LIMITED.
LONDON: SAMUEL BAGSTER & SONS, LIMITED.